BIRNBAUM'S

P9-DFK-865

2015

Walt Disney World For Kids

Wendy Lefkon
Editorial Director

Jill Safro
Editor

Jessica Ward
Contributing Editor

Pam Brandon
Contributing Editor

Clark Wakabayashi
Designer

Alexandra Mayes Birnbaum
Consulting Editor

THE
OFFICIAL
GUIDE

DISNEP EDITIONS

NEW YORK • LOS ANGELES

For Steve, who made all of this possible.

Copyright © 2014 Disney Enterprises, Inc.
All photographs and artwork copyright © 2014 Disney Enterprises, Inc.

Tarzan® is owned by Edgar Rice Burroughs, Inc., and Used by Permission.
All Tarzan materials copyright © 2014 Edgar Rice Burroughs, Inc., and
Disney Enterprises, Inc. All Rights Reserved.

Toy Story characters © Disney Enterprises, Inc./Pixar Animation Studios
A Bug's Life characters © Disney Enterprises, Inc./Pixar Animation Studios

Indiana Jones™ Epic Stunt Spectacular © and Star Tours © Disney/Lucasfilm, Ltd.

Winnie the Pooh characters based on the "Winnie the Pooh" works by
A. A. Milne and E. H. Shepard

The Twilight Zone™ is a registered trademark of CBS, Inc., and is used pursuant to
a license from CBS, Inc.

American Idol® is a registered trademark of 19 TV Ltd. and FremantleMedia
NorthAmerica, Inc.

Cover photograph by Michael Carroll

All rights reserved. Published by Disney Editions, an imprint of Disney Book Group.
No part of this work may be reproduced or transmitted in any form or by any means,
electronic or mechanical, including photocopying, recording, or by any information
storage and retrieval system, without written permission from the publisher. For
information address Disney Editions, 1101 Flower Street, Glendale, California 91201.

ISBN 978-1-4231-9413-2
V381-8386-5-14220

Printed in the United States of America

An enormous debt of gratitude is owed to Alicia Davids, Jonathan Frontado,
Heather Reed Guay, Maureen Hogan, Steven Miller, Karen McClintock, Martina Berry,
Melissa Chilton, Randi Hoffert, Jillian Rowley, Alyse Goodwin, Sara Lamason, Kathleen
Winn, Joanna O'Connell, Paula Wheeler, Chris Ostrander, Nick Hafele, Henry Daubney,
Yadira Ambert, Peggy Arthur, Robert Sias, Liz Marsak. On the photo team, Stacey Cook,
Irene Ferdinand, and Mike Carroll, all of whom performed above and beyond the call
of duty to make the creation of this book possible. And to Phil Lengyel, Tom Elrod,
Linda Warren, Bob Miller, and Charlie Ridgway, thanks for believing in this project
in the first place.

Other 2015 Birnbaum's Official Disney Guides: *Disneyland* and *Walt Disney World*

CONTENTS

You're Going to Disney World!

When you first heard the news, you couldn't believe your ears. Could it be true? Were you really going on a vacation to Walt Disney World? Well, believe it or not, it's true! Before you know it, you'll be in the sunny state of Florida. It's the home of Walt Disney World and the most famous mouse on planet Earth. (Hint: His name starts with M.)

If you have ever been there, you already know that it's one mighty big place with lots to do. In fact, there is so much going on that it can get a little confusing. That's where this book comes in handy. It describes everything in the World, from the Magic Kingdom theme park to the Hoop-Dee-Doo Musical Revue. And it's filled with advice from kids like you.

There is no right or wrong way to read this book. You can start on the first page and read straight through to the end. Or you can skip around, read your favorite parts first, and come back to the rest later.

No matter what you do, one thing is for sure: When you are done, you will be a true-blue Disney expert. Soon kids may start asking *you* for advice on how to have the most awesome vacation at Walt Disney World!

Pack a Pen and
Take Me Along With You

Don't leave this book behind when you head for the parks. It's full of tips and information that you'll want to remember. There are pages for photos and autographs, too — so don't forget to bring a pen and your camera. Here are some ways to use this book while visiting the wonderful world of Disney:

Track Your Trip

Each time you check out an attraction, check it off in this book. Then you'll know what's left to see on your next visit.

Search for Hidden Mickeys

Disney Imagineers have hidden images of Mickey all over Walt Disney World. (Many look like the three connected circles that form Mickey's head.) You might see them in shadows, lights, drawings, or even in the clouds at some attractions. Look in this book for each *Hidden Mickey Alert!* to find a Hidden Mickey clue. Keep track of the number of Hidden Mickeys that you discover. That way when your WDW trip is over, you can write that number on page 141 of this book's Magical Memories section.

Find the Fastpass

Disney's FASTPASS

Would you like to walk to the front of the line at some of the best rides? You can if you have a **Fastpass+** assignment. They are offered for every ride that has a Fastpass symbol by its name in this book. Here's how it works: Reserve a Fastpass in advance with the My Disney Experience app or website (ask a parent for help). You may also get a same-day Fastpass at a station in each theme park. Visit the attraction at your assigned time, and soon you should be on the ride! It is free for all guests — as long as they have a park ticket.

We're Warning You!

Disney rides are full of surprises. That's part of what makes them so much fun. But not everyone likes surprises. So if things like loud noises or fast turns scare you, look at the book's **attraction reaction** warnings before you go on each ride. That way, the only surprises you come across will be good ones!

LOUD
Attraction Reaction

SCARY
Attraction Reaction

WET
Attraction Reaction

DARK
Attraction Reaction

WILD
Attraction Reaction

The last pages of this book are for autographs.

Meet the Readers

What do the kids who helped with this book all have in common? They love Walt Disney World! How do we know? They told us so! Every kid who wrote to us last year received a survey form to fill out. These surveys came back filled with all different opinions about Walt Disney World. The forms also helped us find out about readers' interests and backgrounds.

What did we learn? For starters, a whole lot of you enjoy reading, writing, playing sports, making music, and computers. You also like dancing, singing, and drawing. Your favorite place to stay at Walt Disney World is the Port Orleans Riverside resort. You're not crazy about loud or dark rides. But wild rides like Splash Mountain and Rock 'n' Roller Coaster are at the top of your list. You think Blizzard Beach is the perfect place to spend the day splashing around. And when you can't find a Mickey Mouse Ice Cream Bar to snack on, you love to get popcorn or the frozen pineapple treat called a Dole Whip. Yum!

To everyone who filled out a survey, THANK YOU! This book couldn't have been written without you.

— Jill Safro, Editor

Mickey is Number One!

It's probably not a surprise to hear that Mickey Mouse is still the most popular Disney character with readers. And his best girl, Minnie, is in second place. But who would've guessed that Goofy would be a close third? Gwarsh! Rounding out the top five faves are Donald Duck and Tinker Bell. Who's your favorite? Let us know!

The Magic Kingdom Rules!

More than half of our readers picked the Magic Kingdom as their favorite theme park. Is it yours?

Animal Kingdom 6%
Epcot 12%
Disney's Hollywood Studios 19%
Magic Kingdom 63%

You Love a Wild Ride!

We asked you what types of rides you like best. It turns out most of you like the twists and turns of thrill rides. What daredevils!

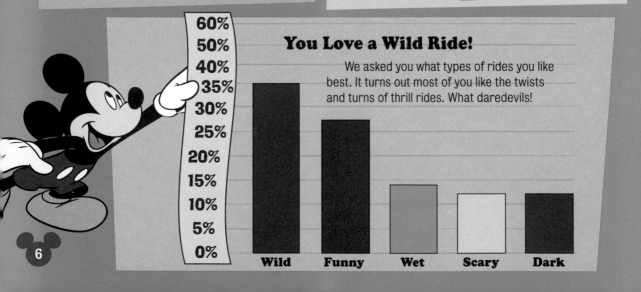

60% 50% 40% 35% 30% 25% 20% 15% 10% 5% 0%

Wild | Funny | Wet | Scary | Dark

Look for this Reader Pleaser ribbon throughout the book. We've placed it beside our readers' ten favorite Disney attractions. If you'd like to cast your vote for next year's Reader Pleasers, write us a letter and we'll send you a survey form. Our address is listed below.

The Reader Review

Every reader who was mailed a survey also got an application to become a Birnbaum Ace Reporter. Their Reader Reviews appear at the many attractions in this book. Use the opinions of the Ace Reporters to decide if the ride is worth the wait or one to skip!

And the Winner is . . .

One lucky Ace Reporter was picked at random to win a special prize. And the winner is . . . Domenica from Woodbridge, Ontario, Canada!

Domenica is 12 years old. Her favorite Walt Disney World attractions are Haunted Mansion and Peter Pan's Flight. Who are on top of her favorite character list? That would be Sulley and Snow White. Domenica enjoys making art, reading, writing, and watching Disney movies. And when it comes to Disney World resorts, she thinks the Yacht Club is tops.

Way to go, Domenica! And thanks for your input to the 2015 edition of Birnbaum's *Walt Disney World For Kids*.

Reader Tip

Keep an eye out for this symbol. Every time you spot it, you'll find a great tip sent in by a reader. Do you have any Walt Disney World tips? We would love to hear them!

What do YOU think?

Do you agree or disagree with any of the kids in this book? Tell us! Send us a letter about your trip and a self-addressed, stamped envelope to the address on the right.

We will send you a survey and read every letter before we write next year's book.

Birnbaum's Disney Guides
Kid Expert Applications

Disney Editions
125 West End Ave.
3rd floor
New York, NY 10023

Meet the Editor

PHOTO BY MIKE CARROLL

Hi. My name's Jill. I'm one of the big kids who helped put this book together. Mickey and Minnie helped us out, too!

Meet Walt Disney

Walt thought of Mickey as his own son.

Walt Disney was born in Illinois on December 5, 1901 — that's more than one hundred years ago! During his life and for all the years after, Walt Disney's company created famous cartoons, movies, theme parks, books, and toys (plus much, much more) for everyone to enjoy . . . but how did it all begin?

When Walt was a little boy, he would look up at the sky and imagine the clouds were animals. As the wind pushed a cloud, a pig would turn into a cow. Soon, the cow would become a chicken! It was then that Walt realized that anything was possible with a little imagination.

But he knew that success would not come from daydreaming alone. Growing up on a farm had taught him the importance of hard work. And it's a good thing, because without Walt's hard work, we would never have met the most famous mouse in the world.

MAGICAL MILESTONES

1901
Walt Disney is born on December 5 in Chicago, Illinois.

1928
Walt creates Mickey Mouse. Mickey stars in his first movie, *Steamboat Willie*.

1937
Walt's animators finish *Snow White and the Seven Dwarfs*, the first full-length animated movie.

1955
Walt's dream to make a family theme park comes true. Disneyland opens in Anaheim.

1971
Walt Disney World (WDW) opens near Orlando, Florida.

1975
Space Mountain, the first WDW roller coaster, opens.

1982
Epcot opens at WDW.

A mouse is born

In 1928, Walt created a little cartoon mouse (Walt almost named him Mortimer Mouse. Luckily, Lilly Disney convinced her husband to name him Mickey Mouse instead!). Mickey's first movie was a black-and-white cartoon called *Steamboat Willie*. It was an instant success. But one hit wasn't enough for its creator. Walt was always looking for new challenges. In 1937, his animation company made the first full-length cartoon movie: *Snow White and the Seven Dwarfs*. Walt was very proud that he had made a movie for everyone in the family to enjoy.

Steamboat Willie was the first talking cartoon ever made.

Family was very important to Walt. Every Saturday, he would do something special with his two daughters. They often went to amusement parks. The kids loved it, but Walt was sad that there weren't rides for parents. *I wish there were a place where children and grown-ups could have fun together,* he thought.

A dream is a wish your heart makes

Since a place like that didn't exist, Walt decided to build it. At first he was going to call it Mickey Mouse Park, but then he named it Disneyland. Disneyland opened in Anaheim, California, in 1955. Families traveled from all over the world to visit it. Disneyland was so popular that Walt's new dream was to build an even bigger park: Disney World. He must have wished upon a star — because his dream came true.

Mickey's birthday is November 18th. When is yours?

1983 Tokyo Disneyland opens in the capital city of Japan.

1989 Disney-MGM Studios opens at WDW.

1992 Disneyland Paris opens in France.

1996 WDW celebrates its 25th anniversary.

2006 Expedition Everest opens in Animal Kingdom.

2008 Toy Story Mania! opens at Disney's Hollywood Studios.

2014 The Seven Dwarfs Mine Train arrives in the Magic Kingdom.

What a
Wonderful World

Walt Disney loved dreaming up stories to tell and new ways to tell them. After he died, his brother Roy kept one of his biggest dreams alive. He made sure Walt's special "world" was built just the way Walt had imagined it. Roy even insisted that it be called *Walt* Disney World, so everyone would know it had been his brother's dream.

Walt Disney World officially opened on October 1, 1971. Since then, millions of people have stopped in for a visit. Some people come to Walt Disney World for a day, but most stay a little longer. There's just so much to see and do.

Pick a theme park, any theme park

The most famous part of Walt Disney World is the **Magic Kingdom**. It's home to Cinderella Castle, Splash Mountain, and those rascally Pirates of the Caribbean. It's also where you can have an adventure with Peter Pan or Winnie the Pooh. Kids of all ages can't get enough of this happy place. Of course, there are three other theme parks to see.

Epcot is a place of science and discovery. Here you can search for Nemo at The Seas with Nemo and Friends. It's also a great place to go on a "world tour" or soar over California. Different countries have shops, restaurants, and attractions inside this park. Epcot opened in 1982.

Are you a showbiz fan? If so, you will get a kick out of **Disney's Hollywood Studios** theme park. It's filled with movie and TV themed rides and exhibits. The secrets of animation are

revealed at The Magic of Disney Animation. Belle and Gaston sing and dance at Beauty and the Beast — Live on Stage. And The Twilight Zone Tower of Terror scares *everybody* silly. Disney's Hollywood Studios opened in 1989.

Disney's Animal Kingdom celebrates the wonders of nature and the creatures that live in it. It got off to a roaring start in 1998. The park has what it takes to make any kid's day: an African safari ride filled with wild animals, dinosaurs that seem real, a roller coaster adventure with a scary abominable snowman, and a super slimy 3-D movie about bugs.

Chill out!

Need to cool off on a hot day? You can make a splash at a Disney water park. Between **Typhoon Lagoon** and **Blizzard Beach**, it's almost impossible to stay dry. Each one has slippery slides, tube rides, and some very cool pools.

But wait — there's more! Walt Disney World also has boats, bikes, and even horses to ride. It has hundreds of restaurants, shops, and other places to explore. In fact, no matter how many times you visit, there's always something new to see. Will Walt Disney World ever be finished? Not as long as there is imagination left in the world. And that's exactly how Walt would have wanted it.

Getting Ready to Go

Planning a vacation to Walt Disney World is lots of fun. But it's not as easy as it sounds. There are so many choices to make! Which parks should you visit? What should you pack? And where can you meet your favorite Disney characters? Use this book to answer these questions and help plan your family's vacation. Remember: It's never too early to get started!

Make a Simple Schedule

Did you know that there are more than 300 attractions at Walt Disney World? It could take weeks to see them all. And most people don't have weeks to spend on vacation. That's why it's important to make a schedule before you leave home. Without it, you might miss some of the rides you want to try the most.

What You'll Need
• Paper   • Pencil   • This book

What to Do

1. Write "Magic Kingdom" at the top of a piece of paper.

2. Look at the Magic Kingdom chapter. Every time you see an attraction that sounds like fun, write its name on the paper.

3. When you have finished the chapter, look over your list. Then put a star next to your ten favorite attractions. These are your "must-sees."

4. Now make a schedule for each of the other theme parks you plan to visit.

5. Don't forget to take your Simple Schedules to the parks!

Learn the Disney Lingo

Audio-Animatronics — Life-like robots, from birds and dinosaurs to movie stars and presidents. They seem real — but they're not.

Cast Member — A Disney employee.

Circle-Vision 360 — A movie that surrounds you. The screens form a circle.

Guidemap — A theme park map that also describes attractions, shops, restaurants, and entertainment.

Imagineer — A creative person who designs Disney attractions.

Save Room for Souvenirs

When you pack for your trip, make sure you're prepared for the weather. Believe it or not, it gets chilly in Florida, especially in the winter. But during the summer it's sizzling hot! It's usually warm during the rest of the year. Layers are a good idea, so you can take something off if you get hot. Remember to pack clothes and shoes that are lightweight and comfortable — since you'll do a lot of walking at the parks. And don't overstuff your suitcase. You may need room for the goodies you get at Walt Disney World.

What else should you bring? That's up to you! Here's a short list to help you get started:

- **A sweatshirt or sweater**
- **Comfy sneakers or shoes**
- **Shorts and pants**
- **Long-sleeved and short-sleeved shirts**
- **A hat and sunglasses**
- **A bathing suit**
- **Sunscreen**

Visit Disney on the Internet

This book is chock-full of information about Disney, but there is another great place to learn about Walt Disney World: the Internet. Visit WDW's website at *www.disneyworld.com*

If you have a question, send an e-mail, and you should get an answer in a few days. If you have a question and don't have access to the Internet, write to:

Walt Disney World
P.O. Box 10000
Lake Buena Vista, FL 32830

COUNTDOWN
TO WALT DISNEY WORLD

10 DAYS

Start to plan a Disney dinner party. Select some of your favorite vacation foods for the menu. Who is on your guest list?

_____
_____
_____

9 DAYS TILL DISNEY

Get to work on your Magic Kingdom Simple Schedule. (Read page 12 to learn how.)

Which ride are you going to go on first?

_____

6 DAYS

Make some Mouse ears — tape strips of paper together to make a loop big enough to fit around your head. Then cut out two circles and tape them to the front of the loop. Make a pair for everyone invited to your party.

5 MORE DAYS

Plan your Disney's Hollywood Studios Simple Schedule. The first two should be almost done by now.

And start packing! (Flip to page 13 for some packing tips.)

2 DAYS TO GO!

It's party time! Set the table to look festive for your special Disney dinner party. After dessert, share your theme park schedules with your family. Remember to wear your Mouse ears!

1 DAY LEFT

Don't stay up too late — tomorrow is the big day!

Take a look at a calendar. On which day does your Walt Disney World vacation begin? Once you find it, count back ten days — that's the day you can start this special countdown.

To do it, simply color in the number for each day as it arrives. Then try the daily activity. Be sure to ask a grown-up for help. You can make up your own special activities, too!

8 DAYS LEFT

Make a list with addresses of everyone you want to send a postcard to. (Don't forget about e-mail addresses for Internet postcards, too.)

7 DAYS

It's time to start your Epcot Simple Schedule. Have you finished your Magic Kingdom schedule yet?

Which Epcot ride do you think sounds best? _____

4 DAYS

Pop some popcorn and watch your favorite Disney movie with your family.

Which flick did you pick?

_____

3 DAYS

Spend some time on your Animal Kingdom Simple Schedule tonight. Finish up schedules for the other parks, too. Which theme park are you going to visit first? _____

You're going to Walt Disney World! Today's the day:

MONTH / DAY / YEAR

Magic Kingdom

PHOTO BY JILL SAFRO

READER Favorite Theme Park PLEASER

When most people hear the words "Walt Disney World," they think of Cinderella Castle, Splash Mountain, and, of course, Mickey Mouse. They are all here in the Magic Kingdom, along with much more. That's why so many kids say the Magic Kingdom is the most special part of the World.

You can spend lots of time in its six lands — Main Street, U.S.A., Adventureland, Frontierland, Liberty Square, Fantasyland, and Tomorrowland. This chapter will help you decide which attractions you want to see first. Then flip back to page 12. It has tips on how to make a simple Magic Kingdom schedule. That way you can organize your park visit and avoid wasting valuable time.

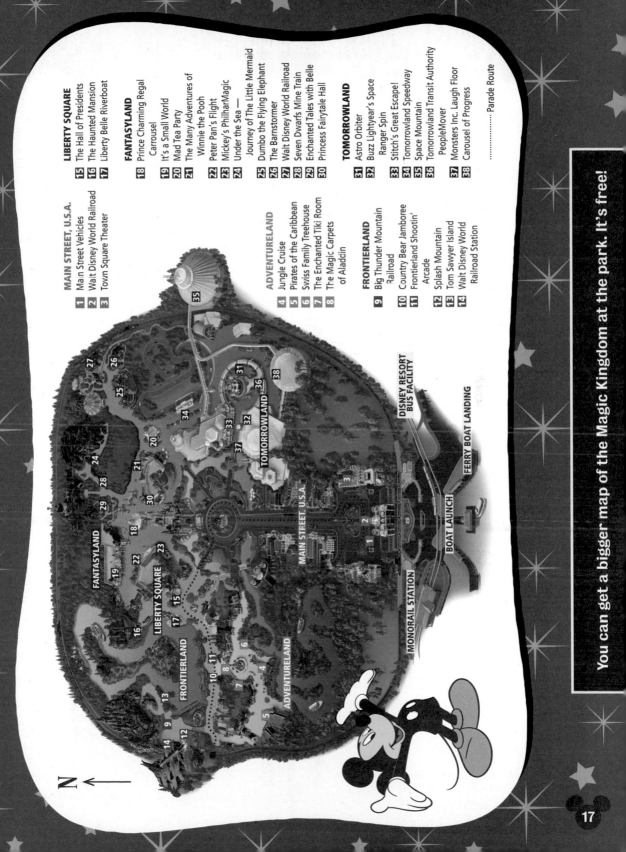

MAIN STREET, U.S.A.
1. Man n Street Vehicles
2. Walt Disney World Railroad
3. Town Square Theater

LIBERTY SQUARE
15. The Hall of Presidents
16. The Haunted Mansion
17. Liberty Belle Riverboat

FANTASYLAND
18. Prince Charming Regal Carrousel
19. It's a Small World
20. Mad Tea Party
21. The Many Adventures of Winnie the Pooh
22. Peter Pan's Flight
23. Mickey's PhilharMagic
24. Under the Sea — Journey of The Little Mermaid
25. Dumbo the Flying Elephant
26. The Barnstormer
27. Walt Disney World Railroad
28. Seven Dwarfs Mine Train
29. Enchanted Tales with Belle
30. Princess Fairytale Hall

ADVENTURELAND
4. Jungle Cruise
5. Pirates of the Caribbean
6. Swiss Family Treehouse
7. The Enchanted Tiki Room
8. The Magic Carpets of Aladdin

FRONTIERLAND
9. Big Thunder Mountain Railroad
10. Country Bear Jamboree
11. Frontierland Shootin' Arcade
12. Splash Mountain
13. Tom Sawyer Island
14. Walt Disney World Railroad Station

TOMORROWLAND
31. Astro Orbiter
32. Buzz Lightyear's Space Ranger Spin
33. Stitch's Great Escape!
34. Tomorrowland Speedway
35. Space Mountain
36. Tomorrowland Transit Authority PeopleMover
37. Monsters Inc. Laugh Floor
38. Carousel of Progress

.... Parade Route

You can get a bigger map of the Magic Kingdom at the park. It's free!

17

Main Street, U.S.A.

Are you ready for some time traveling? You will do a lot of it in the Magic Kingdom. Four out of its six lands send you either back or forward in time.

Main Street, U.S.A., is one of those lands. It was made to look like a small American town in the year 1900. (Some of it is based on the town Walt Disney grew up in — Marceline, Missouri.)

There are pretty lampposts, horse-drawn trolleys, and many other touches that make the street charming. If you look both ways before crossing, you'll notice a big difference between this Main Street and a real one: There's a castle at the end of it!

There are no major attractions here, but Main Street is a fun place to be. You can sink your teeth into a fresh-baked cookie, hop aboard a train, or watch a parade pass by.

Magic Kingdom

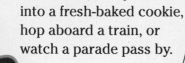

Reader Tip

"The stores on Main Street stay open after the rest of the park closes!"

Greta (age 11)
Brewster, MA

The Reader Review

A Great Big Beautiful Day!

By: Emma, age 12
Deerfield, IL

There's no better cure for sore feet than a trip on the Walt Disney World Railroad. A friendly voice provides information about the park, and there is a nice breeze. It's great for all ages.

Walt Disney World Railroad

Walt Disney loved trains. He even had a miniature one in his backyard that was big enough for him to ride on.

The Magic Kingdom trains are real locomotives that were built nearly a hundred years ago. A full trip takes about 20 minutes, but you can get on or off at any train station (Main Street, U.S.A., Frontierland, or Fantasyland).

What do most kids think about the Magic Kingdom's railroad? They love traveling by train. You get a great view of the park — plus a chance to rest your feet.

HOT TiP!

Town Square Theater is where you can meet Mickey Mouse all day long. You can even get a Fastpass and skip the long line. Bring your camera!

Main Street Vehicles

The Walt Disney World Railroad isn't the only transportation on Main Street, U.S.A. Horse-drawn trolleys, old-fashioned cars, and an antique fire engine make trips up and down the street throughout the day.

You can climb aboard any one of these vehicles in Town Square or by Cinderella Castle. Each trip is strictly one-way — you'll be asked to hop off after the ride.

The vehicles do not operate every day. Stop by City Hall (it's on Main Street) to find out when they are running.

When the horses that pull the trolleys are taking a break, you'll usually find them in the Car Barn near the Emporium. Drop in for a visit.

Hidden Mickey Alert!

Look by the railing around the statue of Walt Disney and Mickey Mouse at the end of Main Street — it casts a Mickey shadow!

Adventureland

A trip to Adventureland is like a visit to a tropical island. It has so many plants and trees that Tarzan would feel right at home. (Don't bother looking for him. He prefers his own treehouse to the one here. It's in Disneyland in California.)

As you can tell from the name of this land, the attractions take you on exciting (and silly) adventures.

Hidden Mickey Alert!

As you enter Adventureland, look at the shields above the bridge. One has a Mickey head carved into it.

PHOTO BY JILL SAFRO

Jungle Cruise

It's a good thing elephants aren't shy. Otherwise, they might get upset when you watch them take a bath. That's just one of the interesting sights on the Jungle Cruise.

The voyage goes through the jungles of Africa and Asia. Along the way you see life-like zebras, giraffes, lions, hippos, and a few headhunters. (Don't worry — the only real animals in the ride are the humans inside the boat!)

The Jungle Cruise is usually very crowded — try to get there early in the morning. It's a good idea to ride during the day, when you can see everything. But if you want a spookier ride, take the cruise at night.

The Reader Review

By: Shawn, age 12
York, PA

I like this ride because of all the corny jokes the captain tells. They're so funny! I liked the animals better when I was younger, but I still ride to hear those famous jokes!

Hidden Mickey Alert!

Keep an eye out for the bathing elephants — a Mickey is carved into the rock behind them.

Hidden Mickey Alert!

Be on the lookout for a singing donkey — his ears cast a Mickey shadow!

HOT TiP!

Do you think you'd make a good pirate? Find out by joining a quest called A Pirate's Adventure — Treasure of the Seven Seas. You will use a map and a magic charm to help find treasure and keep pirate enemies away!

FASTPASS

Pirates of the Caribbean

Dead men tell no tales! That's the warning a pirate gives near the start of this attraction. Don't worry — this classic ride isn't going to hurt you. But there is a small dip and some dark scenes, so be prepared.

The journey takes place in a little boat. After floating through a cave... *BOOM!* You're in the middle of a pirate attack! Cannons blast while the song "Yo Ho, Yo Ho, a Pirate's Life for Me" plays in the background.

The pirates and animals look real. But they are Audio-Animatronics figures (kind of like robots). Look for

a pirate with his leg hanging over a bridge — the leg is really hairy.

In case you didn't know: This is the attraction that inspired Disney's *Pirates of the Caribbean* movies. Arrrrrrr!

The Reader Review

By: Conor, age 10
Cork, Ireland

My favorite part of the ride is the lady chasing the pirates with a broom! My 6-year-old brother was afraid of the pirate battle. It's really not that scary, but it might be better for older kids.

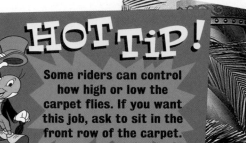

HOT TiP!

Some riders can control how high or low the carpet flies. If you want this job, ask to sit in the front row of the carpet.

The Reader Review

By: Chelsea, age 12
Lincoln University, PA

This is an awesome ride. You get a nice view of other attractions in the area while you are up in the air. Kids of all ages will like this ride.

PHOTO BY JILL SAFRO

The Magic Carpets of Aladdin

If a genie granted you some wishes, what would they be? To be a prince and win the heart of a lovely princess? Well, that was Aladdin's wish, and thanks to his funny friend, Genie, his request came true.

You won't find a real genie at this ride, but you will get to take a high-flying trip on a magic carpet — much like Aladdin and Jasmine did in the animated movie.

The magic touch

Like Dumbo the Flying Elephant in Fantasyland, riders on The Magic Carpets of Aladdin use gears to control their own carpet's flight.

Also like Dumbo, these magic carpets really soar. Beware of the golden camel — he likes to spit at Magic Kingdom guests!

A whole new world

Kids who made a visit to Adventureland before may notice that this land now has a special look. The different shops and decorations make it look a bit like the busy marketplace of Agrabah from *Aladdin*. You might even see the characters from the movie during your visit. So keep a pen handy for autographs when you are in the area.

Swiss Family Treehouse

Before he wrote a book called *The Swiss Family Robinson*, Johann Wyss and his kids imagined what it would be like for their family to be stranded on an island. Together they came up with lots of crazy adventures for the Robinsons. They survive a shipwreck, fight off pirates, and build the most awesome treehouse in the world.

Walt Disney Productions made a movie based on the book in 1960. The Swiss Family Treehouse in Adventureland looks just like the treehouse in the film. In it, you climb a staircase to many different levels. Each room has lots to see. The tree itself looks very real, but it's not. It has 300,000 plastic leaves, and concrete roots.

PHOTO BY MIKE CARROLL

Sorcerers of the Magic Kingdom

Disney villains are trying to take over the Magic Kingdom and you can help defeat them. How? First, Merlin the magician will make you an apprentice sorcerer. Then you can use magic spell cards to beat the bad guys and save the park! The role-playing game starts at the Firehouse on Main Street, U.S.A. Just present your park ticket and you will get a special key card, five magic spell cards, and a map. (It doesn't cost extra to play.) As you follow the clues, you will try to prevent the villains from stealing Merlin's crystal ball. Good luck to you!

Each time you visit the park, you can get more cards — and they are yours to keep. Many kids enjoy collecting and trading the cards as much as they do playing the game.

Reader Tip

"If you like to collect Sorcerers cards, you may find kids willing to trade with you at the portals in the park." (Make sure you have a grown-up with you when you trade cards.)

Kevin (age 8)
Crystal Lake, IL

23

Walt Disney's Enchanted Tiki Room

Birds rule at this attraction. They also sing and crack lots of jokes. If you've been here before, you may know José, Michael, Fritz, and Pierre. They've been singing old favorites like "The Tiki, Tiki, Tiki Room" for more than 40 years.

So what makes this tiki room enchanted? We already know that the birds all sing — but so do the flowers! In fact, even the masks on the wall get in on the act. The show takes place all around you, so don't forget to look up and behind you. And don't worry — there isn't a bad seat in the house. Be sure to warm up your vocal cords before heading to the Tiki Room — the audience is asked to join in and "sing like the birdies sing."

PHOTO BY MIKE CARROLL

Hidden Mickey Alert!

Look for a Mickey or two on the bird perches inside the Tiki Room.

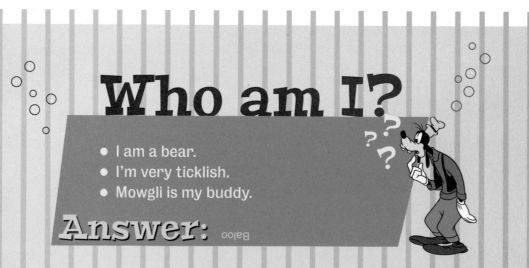

Who am I?

- I am a bear.
- I'm very ticklish.
- Mowgli is my buddy.

Answer: Baloo

Frontierland

Howdy, pardners! And welcome to the Wild West. Frontierland shows you what America was like when pioneers first settled west of the Mississippi River. It's also where you'll find two of the best rides in the Magic Kingdom. Both of them are special Disney mountains. You can take a watery trip down Splash Mountain and ride a runaway train at Big Thunder Mountain Railroad. These are just a few of the fun things to do here.

HOT TiP!

Bring four quarters if you want to play at the Frontierland Shootin' Arcade.

The Reader Review

A Great Big Beautiful Day!

By: Dan, age 12
Hummelstown, PA

I think every kid who comes to the Magic Kingdom should explore Tom Sawyer Island. I would have spent more time there if I could. The caves are the best part.

Tom Sawyer Island

There's only one way to get to Tom Sawyer Island — by raft. That's the way Tom himself used to travel. (Tom Sawyer is a character created by the author Mark Twain.)

Don't expect to find any rides here. In fact, compared to the rest of the Magic Kingdom, it's a pretty calm place. But if you bring your imagination, you can have exciting adventures of your own.

Bouncy bridges and secret exits

The island has a real windmill to wander through, hills to climb, and two bridges. One of them is an old barrel bridge. When one person bounces on it, everyone does. (Hold on to the ropes if you get nervous about falling.)

Across one bridge is a big fort. An Audio-Animatronics blacksmith is working inside it. And there's a secret exit that is really a path through a dark and narrow cave.

In all, there are three caves to explore. They are the best things on the island. Beware: The caves are dark and may be a little scary.

Younger kids love it here

All of Tom Sawyer Island is popular with younger kids. Older kids think the bridges and caves are the best part.

HOT TiP!

If you sit in the front or on the right side of the log, you get really wet!

Hidden Mickey Alert!

Look in the clouds during the final riverboat scene for a sleeping Mickey. (It comes after the big splash.)

The Reader Review A Great Big Beautiful Day!

By: Gregory, age 8
Canonsburg, PA

Splash Mountain is one of my favorite rides because of the scenery. I love following Br'er Rabbit through his adventures. My favorite part is the big drop!

Splash Mountain

DISNEY'S **FASTPASS**

READER **#3** RIDE PLEASER

After riding Splash Mountain, you'll know how it got its name. It's impossible to stay dry! There are three small dips leading up to a giant, watery drop.

You're all wet

No matter which seat you sit in, there's a good chance you'll get wet. But if you sit in the front, you're sure to get soaked. Don't worry, you'll dry off fast in the Florida sun.

The scenery tells the story

Kids agree that you have to go on it a few times before you can understand the ride's story. (You travel through scenes from Walt Disney's movie *Song of the South*.) Br'er Rabbit is trying to get away from Br'er Fox and Br'er Bear. When the rabbit goes over the edge toward the end, you go along for the ride. (Try to keep your eyes open during the big drop — it won't be easy.)

You must be at least 40 inches tall to ride Splash Mountain.

Hidden Mickey Alert!

This Hidden Mickey is a prickly one — it's part of a cactus at Big Thunder's exit.

PHOTO BY JILL SAFRO

WILD Attraction Reaction

Reader Tip

"During the parade is a good time to go on the most popular attractions — their lines will be shorter than usual."

Joe (age 13)
Roanoke, VA

Disney's FASTPASS

Big Thunder Mountain Railroad

READER #7 RIDE PLEASER

Hang on to your hat, because this is one of the wildest rides in the wilderness. The speedy trains zip in, out, and over a huge, rocky mountain. They pass through scenes with real-looking chickens, goats, donkeys, and more.

The swoops and turns make this a thrilling roller coaster, but it's a lot tamer than Space Mountain. It's a ride you can go on again and again and see new things each time. Look for funny sights in the town — like the poor guy floating around in a bathtub. Try to ride during the day and again at night.

You must be at least 40 inches tall to ride Big Thunder Mountain.

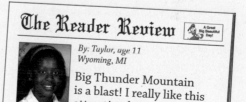

The Reader Review

A Great Big Beautiful Day!

By: Taylor, age 11
Wyoming, MI

Big Thunder Mountain is a blast! I really like this attraction because it doesn't have a lot of dips. I think older kids would like it best — the hard turns might shock younger ones. What makes this ride seem very scary is the hard stop it comes to at the end.

Country Bear Jamboree

You have never seen bears quite like these. They sing songs, play instruments, and tell jokes. This is a silly show, so go in with a silly attitude. Big Al is one of the most popular bears. And he can't even carry a tune!

Everyone gets in on the act

Sometimes the audience sings and claps along with the performers. Even the furry heads on the wall get into the act. (Melvin the moose, Buff the buffalo, and Buck the deer like to hang around the theater.)

What do kids think of the bears?

The kooky country music show gets mixed reviews from kids. Some love it.

Others aren't so thrilled. But almost everyone agrees that younger kids seem to enjoy it the most. It's also a great place to cool off and rest up on a hot day.

The Reader Review

By: Matthew, age 11
Peachtree City, GA

Country Bear Jamboree is not that interesting to me because I am not that into country music. I wish it had more talking and less singing. The show is okay because it is funny. The bears tell some pretty silly jokes!

Liberty Square

Hidden Mickey Alert!

The gravestones in one of The Haunted Mansion's last rooms bear tiny three-circle Mickeys.

What did America look like in Colonial days? Parts of it looked like Liberty Square! This small area separates Frontierland from Fantasyland. It's a quiet spot with some shops and a couple of popular attractions.

READER RIDE PLEASER #9

Disney's FASTPASS

DARK Attraction Reaction

SCARY Attraction Reaction

The Haunted Mansion

This haunted house isn't too scary, but there are plenty of ghosts to keep you on your toes. Before you enter, enjoy the interactive wait area and read the funny tombstones outside. (We like the one that says: HERE LIES GOOD OLD FRED. A GREAT BIG ROCK FELL ON HIS HEAD.)

Once inside, you'll be stranded in a room with no windows and no doors. For a while, it seems like there's no way out.

There's a moment before you board a "Doom Buggy" when the room is totally dark. It's just a few seconds, but for some, it's too long.

The car doesn't move very fast, but it is still hard to catch all the details. Watch for the door knockers that knock all by themselves, a ghostly teapot pouring tea, and a ghost napping under the table at a party in the old ballroom.

The Reader Review

A Great Big Beautiful Day!

By: Domenica, age 12
Woodbridge, Ontario, Canada

The Haunted Mansion is my all-time favorite ride. The first time I went I was scared. If you're scared, don't worry— the happy haunts are there to make you laugh. This ride is super fun for the whole family. (But some little kids may get spooked.)

The Hall of Presidents

The first part of this attraction is a film about U.S. government. Then the screen rises and all of the American presidents are on stage together. They are Audio-Animatronics, but they look real. How many presidents can you name in the photo below?

During the show, some presidents actually speak. (President Barack Obama recorded his own voice. Abraham Lincoln and George Washington are voiced by actors.) If you watch closely, you'll notice the presidents move and whisper. They all seem real!

The Reader Review

A Great Big Beautiful Day!

By: Amy, age 11
Toms River, NJ

It's amazing how real the presidents look. Kids interested in history will really enjoy the show, but others might find it too long.

Liberty Belle Riverboat

The *Liberty Belle* riverboat docks in Liberty Square. This big steamboat takes guests on slow, relaxing cruises. It can be a nice break on a busy day (though there aren't many seats). The best spots are right up front or in the back, where you can see both sides of the river as you float along.

PHOTO BY JILL SAFRO

Fantasyland

Fantasyland is home to a lot of magical rides that younger kids just love. Older kids and even grown-ups enjoy them, too. These attractions are very popular, and the waits can be long. But the lines are usually a bit shorter while people are watching the afternoon parade. So it's a good idea to skip the parade one day and spend time in Fantasyland. Plan to catch the parade on another day.

Prince Charming Regal Carrousel

Just about all of the attractions at Walt Disney World were dreamed up by Disney Imagineers. But not this carrousel. It was discovered in New Jersey, where it was once part of another amusement park. It was built around 1917.

When you climb on a horse for your ride on the carrousel, be sure to notice that each horse is different. And remember to look up at the ceiling and its handpainted scenes from *Cinderella*. While you ride, listen for famous Disney tunes, including "When You Wish Upon a Star" and "Be Our Guest."

Reader Tip

"If you want to meet Cinderella, have a meal at Cinderella's Royal Table in the castle. She'll be in the lobby!" (You can also meet her in Fantasyland at Princess Fairytale Hall.)

Christine (age 10)
Horsham, PA

Mad Tea Party

The idea for the giant teacups that spin through this ride came from a famous scene in *Alice in Wonderland*. In the movie, the Mad Hatter throws himself a tea party to celebrate his un-birthday. That's any day of the year that isn't his birthday!

On the Mad Tea Party ride, you control how fast your cup spins by turning the big wheel in the center. The more you turn, the more you spin. Or you can just sit back and let the cup spin on its own. It may be hard while you're whirling, but try to take a peek at the little mouse that keeps popping out of the big teapot in the center.

The Reader Review

By: Elizabeth, age 11
Jackson, GA

This ride is fun for the whole family. It's best when everyone helps spin. But if you get dizzy easily, don't turn the wheel, and try not to look outside of your cup as it spins!

The Barnstormer

The wildest ride in Fantasyland is a roller coaster in Storybook Circus. This ride may look small, but it packs plenty of thrills. It takes you on a twisting and turning flight high above the park.

The trip starts out slow, but watch out! Before you know it, you will be swooping and soaring through the circus. Hang on tight!

Before you board, be sure to check out the magical area surrounding the ride — that Goofy really is quite goofy! You must be at least 35 inches tall to ride this mini roller coaster.

PHOTO BY JILL SAFRO

The Reader Review

By: Becca, age 12
Weston, FL

This ride isn't only for little kids. I still ride it every time I go to the Magic Kingdom. It's a great way to experience your first roller coaster.

Dumbo the Flying Elephant

Disney's FASTPASS

Just like the star of the movie *Dumbo*, these elephants know how to fly. They'd love to take you for a short ride (about two minutes) above Fantasyland. A button lets you control the up-and-down movement of the elephant.

Take your kid brother or sister

Many kids agree that this ride is more fun for younger kids, from ages 3 to 8. But they all find something to like and think it would be fun to go on with a younger brother or sister.

Beware of long lines

Even though Dumbo has doubled in size (so more people can ride), the lines for this attraction tend to be long. Get a Fastpass if you can. If not, head to Dumbo as soon as you get to the Magic Kingdom. If the line is already too long when you get there, try again toward the end of the day, when the youngest kids may have already gone home.

HOT TiP!

Need to cool off? Or do you just enjoy jumping in puddles? Head to the Casey Junior Splash 'N' Soak Station. You'll be glad you did!

PHOTO BY JILL SAFRO

Magic Kingdom

The Reader Review

A Great Big Beautiful Day!

By: Rachel, age 10
Franklin, TN

I think this ride is more fun if you go on it with your little brother or sister. I like that you can control how high or low you want to be.

HOT TiP!

Would you like to meet Disney princesses? Head to Princess Fairytale Hall! Royal folks such as Elsa, Rapunzel, and Cinderella greet guests all day long.

Peter Pan's Flight

Swoop and soar through scenes that tell the story of how Wendy, Michael, and John get sprinkled with pixie dust and fly off to Never Land with Peter Pan and Tinker Bell. Along the way, you see Princess Tiger Lily, Captain Hook, and Hook's sidekick, Mr. Smee.

Near the beginning of the trip, there's a beautiful scene of London at night. Notice that the cars on the streets really move. Later, watch out for the crocodile that wants to eat Captain Hook.

When you first board your pirate ship, it seems like you're riding on a track on the ground. Once you get going, the track is actually above you, so it feels like the ship is really flying.

The Reader Review

By: Rich, age 13
Palm Harbor, FL

This attraction is amazing. No wonder the line is so long! It makes you feel as if you are really flying over London. You can see tiny cars and buildings on the ground. I recommend this ride for all ages.

PHOTO BY JILL SAFRO

Hidden Mickey Alert!

Many Mickeys can be found in the vines you see in the African scene.

PHOTO BY JILL SAFRO

"it's a small world"

It's a Small World

DISNEY'S FASTPASS

People have a lot in common, no matter where they live. That's the point of this attraction. In it, you take a slow boat ride through several large rooms where singing dolls represent different parts of the world. There are Greek dancers, Japanese kite flyers, Scottish bagpipers, and many more. There's also a jungle scene with hippos, giraffes, and monkeys.

All this colorful scenery is set to the song "It's a Small World, After All."

The signs at the end all say good-bye in a different language. *Aloha! Shalom! Sayonara! Adios!*

The Reader Review

A Great Big Beautiful Day!

By: Maggie, age 11
Lee's Summit, MO

Nobody should pass up this classic attraction! I love seeing all the different cultures and guessing where the dolls come from. All ages will enjoy It's a Small World.

Reader Tip

"Get your Fastpass early in the day. They might be all given away by evening!"

Christopher (age 11)
Valley View, OH

DISNEP'S FASTPASS

The Many Adventures of Winnie the Pooh

Winnie the Pooh loves his honey. In fact, he'll do anything to keep the sweet treat safe. On this trip through the Hundred Acre Wood, see what Pooh must do to rescue his honey pots and his friends, too.

The blustery day

The wind is howling, the leaves are rustling, and everything in Pooh's world is blowing away. Roo and Piglet are up in the air. And Owl's house is about to topple over. Hold on tight, or you just might be swept away next!

A sticky situation

Finally the wind calms and Pooh can get to sleep. But when he wakes up from his silly dream, it's raining outside. Pooh's honey pots are about to wash away. He can save them, but will he save himself? Keep in mind that some kids think the interactive wait area is as much fun as the attraction itself. Be sure to check it out!

The Reader Review *A Great Big Beautiful Day!*

By: Ryan, age 11
Milford, MA

My family and I love this ride. My favorite part is when you bounce like Tigger. Get a Fastpass because the line can get very long. You don't want to be saying, "Oh, bother."

Under the Sea — Journey of The Little Mermaid

This attraction invites you to join Ariel for a colorful adventure. Are you ready to dive in? You'll go "under the sea" by boarding a special vehicle called a clam-mobile. (They are giant shells, like the ones over at The Seas with Nemo and Friends in Epcot.) And don't worry about getting wet — the water here is just a cool special effect.

Once you board your clam-mobile, the journey begins. Along the way, you'll meet up with Ariel, Flounder, and all of their pals. There is a lot to see and hear in this attraction — you may have to ride it twice to take it all in!

PHOTO BY JILL SAFRO

The Seven Dwarfs Mine Train

Are you ready to journey into the mine where a million diamonds shine? Then head to the Seven Dwarfs Mine Train! The brand-new attraction is a roller coaster ride with a twist — the cars move up and down along the track *and* they sway from side to side!

Heigh ho, heigh ho!

If you have seen Disney's *Snow White and the Seven Dwarfs*, you know where Sleepy, Dopey, Doc, and their friends work — in a diamond mine. At this attraction, guests board train cars and visit that colorful mine.

Hang on tight

It's not as speedy as Space Mountain, or as rough as the big drop in Splash Mountain, but this ride can spook some kids. If the Barnstormer is too scary for you, skip this attraction. You must be at least 38 inches tall to ride.

Mickey's PhilharMagic

It's magical. It's musical. It's three-dimensional. It's Mickey's PhilharMagic!

Mickey Mouse is the star of this 3-D movie, but it's not a one-mouse show. Mickey is joined by characters such as Donald Duck, Ariel, Aladdin, Jasmine, and Simba. (Simba starred in the attraction that used to be here: The Legend of the Lion King.)

A one and a two and a three-D

The show takes place in a grand concert hall. Once guests (that's you!) find seats and put on special 3-D glasses, it's showtime.

Sit back, relax, and enjoy as the cast of characters show off their musical talents. (Some are more talented than others.) And be sure to keep your eyes and ears open — a whole lot happens at the same time.

Eye-popping 3-D effects take place on the oversize screen. Music fills the air. And special surprises happen inside the theater.

What's a PhilharMagic?

In case you were wondering . . . Walt Disney World made up the word PhilharMagic. It's based on the real word *philharmonic*, which describes a bunch of musicians who all play their instruments at the same time.

The Reader Review

A Great Big Beautiful Day!

By: Megan, age 9
Quincy, IL

Wow! Aladdin and Jasmine fly over your head in this amazing attraction. Lots of other characters pop off the screen, too. Put this on your list of shows to see!

Enchanted Tales with Belle

Would you like to help Belle tell "the tale as old as time" — the story of Beauty and the Beast? You are invited to her dad's cottage to do just that. The experience starts by taking a step through a big, magical mirror. It transports guests all the way to Beast's castle! There you will meet Madame Wardrobe and her assistant. Together they will assign roles to audience members — be sure to wave your hand when they ask for volunteers. Once all the roles are assigned, guests walk to the library. Expect to be greeted by Lumiere, the friendly candlestick from *Beauty and the Beast*. When Belle arrives, it's story time. This is a very popular attraction and the long line moves slowly. Get a Fastpass if you can.

Tomorrowland

Tomorrowland began as a view of the future. But as the real world changed, so did this land. Now, it's like a city from a science-fiction story. The palm trees are made of metal. The rides here let you rocket through space or zoom through the Magic Kingdom sky. And a silly alien even pops in for a visit! A good way to see this land is to ride on the Tomorrowland Transit Authority — it's relaxing and it never has a long line. And even though you won't have a driver's license until the future, you can drive a car in Tomorrowland (as long as you are at least 54 inches tall).

Tomorrowland Transit Authority PeopleMover

This slow-moving ride travels by or through many Tomorrowland attractions. You will even get a peek at Buzz Lightyear's Space Ranger Spin. But pay attention, because you pass by the window very quickly. You'll also go through Space Mountain, but you won't see much because it's totally dark.

This ride is a good one to head to when it's really hot outside. The cars move just fast enough to create a nice breeze. It's also interesting to know that the ride doesn't make any pollution.

HOT TiP!

If the park is crowded or you need to rest your feet, go to Tomorrowland Transit Authority. The line is short and it moves quickly.

Space Mountain

Disney's FASTPASS

Thrill seekers head straight for this rocket ride through outer space. It has twists, turns, and a few steep dips. And it all takes place in the dark! Space Mountain is one of the most popular rides in Walt Disney World.

READER #4 RIDE PLEASER

SCARY Attraction Reaction
DARK Attraction Reaction
WILD Attraction Reaction

Reader Tip

"For the shortest lines, be there when the park opens!"

Whitney (age 12)
Mount Pleasant, MI

Who turned out the lights?

It's so dark inside Space Mountain that you barely see where you are going — especially if you sit in the front of the rocket. That's what makes the ride so exciting. Every curve comes as a surprise.

You will hear sounds of other rockets zooming by. But don't worry. The coaster is perfectly safe. The noises are meant to add to the excitement.

Is it too scary?

There's no doubt about it: Space Mountain is scary. But some kids say it's a "good scary." The rockets only travel about 28 miles per hour, but it feels much faster. You must be at least 44 inches tall to ride.

The Reader Review

A Great Big Beautiful Day!

By: Erin, age 12
Barrington, IL

This is one of my all-time favorite rides in Disney World! You are completely in the dark, so you can't see *anything*. You don't know when you are going to turn or drop! Unless you're afraid of the dark (or roller coasters), I recommend Space Mountain.

16

Walt Disney's Carousel of Progress

A lot has changed since the year 1900. Most homes had no electricity, water came from a well, and nobody had a TV. Life was rough! This attraction shows how American family life has changed since then.

The show is really four short plays. And the performers are all Audio-Animatronics actors. After each scene, the theater moves to the right. That's when you will hear the song "There's a Great, Big, Beautiful Tomorrow." Feel free to sing along.

Some kids may find the show a bit on the slow side, but others think it's quite special. Why? It was introduced to the world by Walt Disney himself. The special event didn't happen at Disney World (it wasn't open yet), but at the World's Fair in New York City in 1964. Of course, the attraction has been updated (there has been a lot of progress since then), but the show is still an amusing look at American life. And the Carousel of Progress has made history, too — it's had more performances than any other show in the history of American theater.

The Reader Review

By: Faith, age 10
Torrington, CT

This is one of my family's favorite attractions. I recommend it for when you need to take a break from all the excitement and relax.

Who am I?

- I am a rodent.
- I have a black nose.
- Dale is my pal.

Answer: Chip

Stitch's Great Escape!

There is a cuddly alien prisoner who needs guarding. Do you think you can keep him from escaping? Even if the alien is that mischievous rascal named Stitch? This silly attraction asks Magic Kingdom guests to keep an eye on the little guy and keep him out of trouble.

Good luck!

Of course, Stitch rarely does what he's told. When he does escape, his wacky antics keep everyone laughing. And the special effects make it seem like the little

alien is running around the room. Don't be surprised if he sneaks up beside you, whispers in your ear, and musses your hair. (He doesn't have very good manners.)

Stitch can escape, but you can't!

Don't be alarmed when a harness comes down as the show starts. It's just there to make the effects more special. It will lift up automatically at the end of the adventure. (Be sure to sit up straight when it first comes down and let it tap your shoulders.) Everyone must be at least 40 inches tall to enter Stitch's Great Escape.

PHOTO BY JILL SAFRO

The Reader Review

By: Jacob, age 12
Voorhees, NJ

I like to join the cute, blue alien in this fun-filled attraction. It's my favorite show! I think it is good for all ages (unless you're afraid of the dark). If you are a kid reading this now, you should give it a try. You will laugh for sure!

Hidden Mickey Alert!

Watch the planets carefully as they whiz by during the short movie. One of them is extra special — it has a Mickey on it!

HOT TiP!

To get more points on the Buzz Lightyear ride, hold the button down the whole time and aim at small, moving, or faraway targets.

Magic Kingdom

Buzz Lightyear's Space Ranger Spin

In this attraction, everyone is a toy — including you. In fact, you are so small, you fit inside a video game shooting gallery.

To infinity and beyond!

The ride is under the command of Buzz Lightyear. You've just become a Junior Space Ranger, so you're under his command, too. Together, you battle the evil Emperor Zurg.

Zap that Zurg

Zurg and his robots are stealing batteries from other toys. They plan to use the batteries to power their ultimate weapon of destruction. Your job is to fight back. Use the laser cannons in your spaceship to aim at the targets (they look like Zs) and zap Zurg's power. Every time you hit a target, you earn more points. There is a scoreboard next to the laser cannon that keeps track of your points.

At the end of the ride, you'll pass a chart. It shows everyone's ranger rank based on their score. Check to see where your score falls. Most kids improve with practice.

The Reader Review

A Great Big Beautiful Day!

By: Lydia, age 13
Sutton, MA

Everyone will love this ride — it feels like you are in a video game! And you get better at it every time you go on. I think this is the coolest ride in the Magic Kingdom. I recommend getting a Fastpass.

Monsters, Inc. Laugh Floor

Stitch has some new neighbors here in Tomorrowland — Mike, Roz, and other kooky characters from the hit movie *Monsters, Inc.* They are all part of a silly attraction that lets you interact with your animated friends. That's right, the audience members not only watch the show — they are a part of it! Don't worry. The monsters don't want to make kids scream (the way they did in the movie). This time, they want to make kids laugh. So be prepared for lots of wackiness and a bunch of very bad jokes!

The Reader Review

By: Olivia, age 8
West Columbia, SC

This is a very funny attraction. I like that the audience can send in jokes. I was scared that they would put me on the screen and talk to me. I just wanted to watch the show and laugh!

Who am I?

- I can fly.
- Hangman's Tree is my secret hideout.
- I won't grow up!

Answer: Peter Pan

HOT TiP!

Do you have a little brother or sister? Take them on this ride. Young kids love it!

Reader Tip

"If you get lost, don't worry. Just go to the nearest cast member (a worker wearing a name tag) and ask for help."

Sam (age 9)
Eatontown, NJ

Disney's FASTPASS

Tomorrowland Speedway

You don't need a license to drive your own car around this racetrack (as long as you're at least 54 inches tall). Cars travel along a track, but it's not as easy to drive as it looks. Even experts bounce around a lot. The cars are real and are powered by gasoline.

The Reader Review

A Great Big Beautiful Day!

By: Lauren, age 12
Harrisburg, PA

I love this ride. No matter what your age (if you are at least 54 inches tall) you can drive your parents for once! The race track is nice and long. The line to ride is long, too — but it's worth the wait.

Magic Kingdom

Reader Tip

"If you're afraid of heights, skip Astro Orbiter!"

Derek (age 13)
Spokane, WA

Astro Orbiter

In the middle of Tomorrowland, there is a giant, glowing tower. It is called Rockettower. The Astro Orbiter ride is all the way at the top. In it, you soar past colorful planets high above Tomorrowland.

Like on Dumbo the Flying Elephant, you control how high or low your rocket flies. You can ride by yourself or with a friend. (Each rocket fits two people.) But if you want to be the one to control how high you go, be sure to sit in the front.

The Reader Review
A Great Big Beautiful Day!

By: Matthew, age 13
Lakeland, FL

I love going on this ride! Some kids may be scared, but older kids will probably like it best because it goes up very high and tilts when you reach the top.

Entertainment

The Magic Kingdom is a very entertaining place. It seems like there is always a show starting or a parade going by. Read on to learn about some of the special events that take place in the park. For more information, check a park Times Guide. You can get one at the entrance to any Disney theme park, or in the park's shops and restaurants.

MAIN STREET ELECTRICAL PARADE

This nighttime parade makes its way down Main Street, U.S.A., during busy seasons. Special lighting effects and lots of characters make for a great show. This parade does not run every day. Check a park Times Guide for the schedule.

The Reader Review
By: Christopher, age 9
North Easton, MA

What a thrilling sight! You see characters from many different Disney movies. And everything lights up in the night. Get your spot early — it gets crowded for this parade.

DREAM ALONG WITH MICKEY

Do you believe in dreams? You will after you watch this toe-tapping musical show in front of Cinderella Castle. In it, Mickey Mouse and his friends celebrate happy dreams and fight off a nightmare or two (thanks to that nasty Maleficent). The show happens every day.

FESTIVAL OF FANTASY PARADE

Disney characters star in this afternoon parade. You might even get to dance with some characters as they pass by. Be sure to line up early to get a good spot on the curb.

WISHES

Look — up in the sky! It's not a bird or a plane . . . it's an amazing fireworks show! For the best view of the show, stand right in the middle of Main Street, facing the castle.

Where to find
Characters
at the MAGIC KINGDOM

Characters greet guests all over the park. A great place to meet Mickey Mouse is Main Street's **Town Square Theater**. Lots of different characters greet guests on **Main Street** throughout the day. Looking for Disney princesses? Go straight to **Princess Fairytale Hall** in Fantasyland. Minnie, Daisy, Goofy, and Donald hang out at **Pete's Silly Sideshow** in the **Storybook Circus** part of Fantasyland.

Aladdin and Jasmine greet guests in **Adventureland**. Alice and her Wonderland friends prefer **Fantasyland**, while Br'er Rabbit and Br'er Bear enjoy spending time near Splash Mountain in **Frontierland**.

When you're in **Tomorrowland**, keep an eye out for Buzz Lightyear and Stitch.

Frontierland is a good place to catch up with Woody, Jessie, and Bullseye.

Merida from *Brave* mingles with guests in the **Fairytale Garden** (next to Cinderella Castle).

Another way to see Disney pals is at parades and shows. Check a park Times Guide for schedules.

Magic Kingdom

Head to this park first, since it has the most rides for kids.

Arrive a half hour before the opening time. Walk down Main Street to get a head start before the rest of the park opens.

Go to Enchanted Tales with Belle as soon as the park opens. It is a very popular attraction and has one of the longest lines.

Visit Mickey Mouse in the Town Square Theater on Main Street. You can use page 142 of this book for his autograph. And don't forget your camera! (Your parents can buy pictures from Disney's Photopass, too.)

Need to cool off on a hot day? Get wet at Casey Junior Splash 'N' Soak Station in Fantasyland. Or hop on the PeopleMover and enjoy the breeze.

If the park is open late, it's fun to go on your favorite attractions again after dark.

There are "chicken exits" in the lines for all scary rides, just in case you change your mind about riding at the last minute.

Do not eat just before riding The Barnstormer, The Seven Dwarfs Mine Train, Space Mountain, Big Thunder Mountain Railroad, or the Mad Tea Party.

If you've never been on a roller coaster, ride The Barnstormer first. If you enjoy it, try Seven Dwarfs Mine Train — but remember, it is a little scarier!

If there are two lines at an attraction, the one on the left is usually shorter.

Attraction Ratings

COOL
(Check It Out)

- Country Bear Jamboree
- Monsters, Inc. Laugh Floor
- Prince Charming Regal Carrousel
- Tomorrowland Transit Authority PeopleMover
- Liberty Belle Riverboat
- Swiss Family Treehouse
- Walt Disney's Enchanted Tiki Room
- Walt Disney's Carousel of Progress
- Walt Disney World Railroad
- The Hall of Presidents

REALLY COOL
(Don't Miss)

- Astro Orbiter
- Tomorrowland Speedway
- Mad Tea Party
- Jungle Cruise
- Mickey's PhilharMagic
- Dumbo the Flying Elephant
- Enchanted Tales with Belle
- The Magic Carpets of Aladdin
- Stitch's Great Escape!
- Tom Sawyer Island
- The Barnstormer
- Under the Sea — Journey of The Little Mermaid

THE COOLEST
(See at Least Twice)

- Splash Mountain
- Big Thunder Mountain Railroad
- The Haunted Mansion
- Peter Pan's Flight
- Buzz Lightyear's Space Ranger Spin
- Pirates of the Caribbean
- The Many Adventures of Winnie the Pooh
- Space Mountain
- It's a Small World
- Main Street Electrical Parade
- The Seven Dwarfs Mine Train

What do YOU think?

The kids who helped with this book rated all the attractions at Walt Disney World. But your opinion counts, too! Make your own "Attraction Ratings" list for each park and send it to us. We will use it when we create next year's book. (Our address is on page 7.)

Where's Mickey?

Disney Imagineers have hidden Mickey's image all over the Magic Kingdom. Here are a few places to search for Hidden Mickeys while you are in the park. If you want to meet Mickey in person, go to the Town Square Theater. He's there all day!

The Haunted Mansion

In the ghost party room, check out the bottom of the banquet table. There is a Hidden Mickey made out of two saucers and a plate.

Tomorrowland Transit Authority PeopleMover

After passing the Metro Retro Society, look to the right. There you'll see a lady getting her hair done. What's on her belt? A Hidden Mickey!

Buzz Lightyear's Space Ranger Spin

Once you enter the Buzz building, look for a poster on the right and find the planet called Pollost Prime. One of the continents on the map forms Mickey's profile. And keep your eyes open during the attraction's space video scene (about halfway through). You'll see this same planet fly by on the right.

Carousel of Progress

There are a few Hidden Mickeys in this attraction's Christmas scene. Our favorite is the one on top of the fireplace. It's a Mickey nutcracker! Can you find others?

It's a Small World

During the ride, pay close attention in the Africa room. If you search the purple leaves on the ceiling, you may spot several Hidden Mickeys. (They are close to the giraffes.)

Epcot is a great place to make discoveries about the world. At this theme park, things that used to seem ordinary suddenly become fun. All of the attractions at Epcot are in buildings called pavilions (pronounced: *puh-VILL-yuhnz*). The pavilions are in two sections of the park. One section is Future World, and the other is World Showcase. Future World celebrates inventions and ideas. It shows how they affect everything, from the land, sea, sky, and outer space to your home and safety.

World Showcase lets you travel around the world without leaving the park! There are many different countries to visit here. Each country has copies of its famous buildings, restaurants, and other landmarks. Together, they make you feel as if you're visiting the real place.

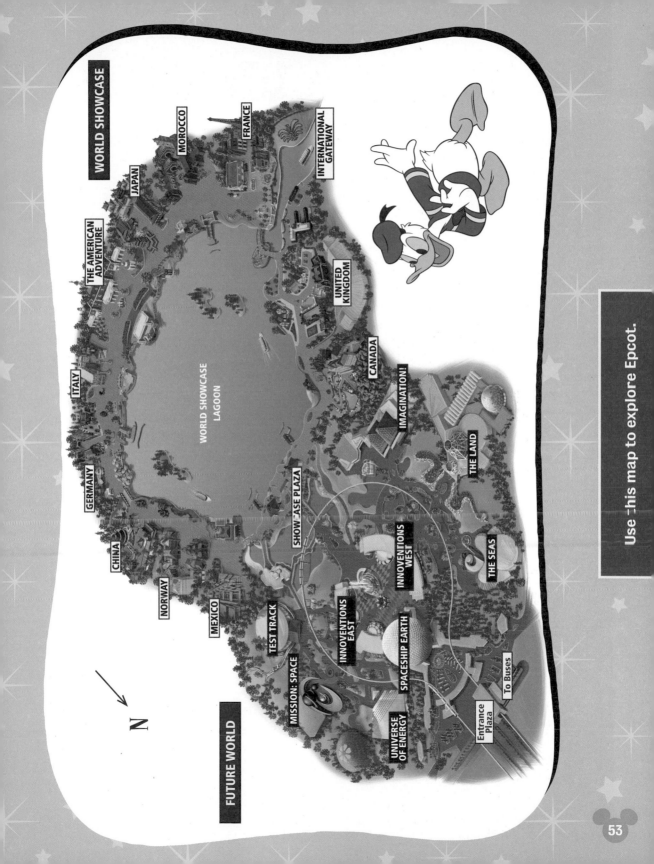

WORLD SHOWCASE

MOROCCO

FRANCE

JAPAN

INTERNATIONAL
GATEWAY

THE AMERICAN
ADVENTURE

UNITED
KINGDOM

ITALY

CANADA

WORLD SHOWCASE
LAGOON

IMAGINATION!

GERMANY

THE LAND

CHINA

THE SEAS

NORWAY

INNOVENTIONS
WEST

MEXICO

SHOWCASE PLAZA

INNOVENTIONS
EAST

TEST TRACK

SPACESHIP EARTH

N

MISSION: SPACE

UNIVERSE
OF ENERGY

Entrance
Plaza

To Buses

FUTURE WORLD

Use this map to explore Epcot.

53

Future World

PHOTO BY JILL SAFRO

When you enter Epcot by monorail, you are in the area called Future World. Many of the attractions here are educational — but that doesn't mean you won't have fun. Take it from other kids: There's a lot to discover.

Reader Tip

"The line for Spaceship Earth is usually shortest toward the end of the day!"

Kersie (age 12)
Vancouver, WA

SPACESHIP EARTH

DARK Attraction Reaction

DISNEY's FASTPASS

You can't miss the giant silver ball that is the symbol of Epcot. It's gigantic! The Spaceship Earth ride is inside this big, round building. (It's called a geosphere.) The attraction explores the ways people have shaped the future throughout history. You'll have a chance to create your own vision of the future. How? By using a touch screen inside your ride vehicle.

The journey takes place in slow-moving time machine vehicles. When the ride is over, you can visit the "Project Tomorrow" area. It's filled with interactive exhibits.

The Reader Review
A Great Big Beautiful Day!

By: Amy, age 12
Clinton, NJ

Some people think this ride is not worth a long wait, but it's one of my family's favorites. It may be a calm ride, but I think it's very interesting. It's a classic!

MISSION: SPACE

The Reader Review *A Great Big Beautiful Day!*

By: Danny, age 12
Chesapeake, VA

This is one of the most unusual rides in Disney World. If you're planning to be an astronaut when you grow up, don't miss it. Mission SPACE is a blast!

FASTPASS

Epcot

Three . . . two . . . one . . . blast-off! This ride lets you know what it's like to be an astronaut on a trip to outer space. In this case, you are on a mission to Mars.

Each spacecraft holds four guests. Once aboard, it's time for take-off. You will really feel the tug of gravity during the launch — just like on a NASA spacecraft. This part lasts nearly a minute, so be ready.

What's your job?

Once you're on your way, things calm down a bit. That may be when you realize you have a job to do. Are you the commander, engineer, pilot, or navigator? That depends on where you sit. It doesn't matter — all the jobs are fun to do. Just before

you land, you will get a strange sensation. It's not weightlessness, but it is definitely out of this world. It's a lot like the feeling astronauts get in outer space.

Mission accomplished

If bouncing or spinning makes you sick, skip the "intense" Orange Team trip — a lot of people get woozy on it. Some even feel sick afterward. You can take a tamer trip to Mars — just ask for the "less intense" Green Team ride at the entrance. You must be at least 44 inches tall to ride either version. If you prefer to skip the attraction, be sure to check the Advanced Training Lab near the Mission SPACE exit. It's got activities that are out of this world!

THE SEAS WITH NEMO & FRIENDS

The Reader Review

A Great Big Beautiful Day!

By: Lauren, age 14
Deerfield Beach, FL

My family and I spent hours at this pavilion. The ride is superb and is home to thousands of gorgeous fish. Be sure to check out the manatees. They're adorable!

It's easy to find Nemo these days — he's at The Seas pavilion at Epcot! He and his friends can't wait for you to visit. There are more than 2,000 real sea creatures living here. There's also a cool ride, a play area, and interesting sea-related exhibits to explore.

The Seas with Nemo & Friends

Jump inside a clam-mobile and let the adventure begin. It's a class trip run by Nemo's teacher, Mr. Ray. It seems little Nemo has wandered off again. Your job is to help find him. Expect to meet up with Dory, Bruce, Chum, Crush, Squirt, and others along the way. And don't worry — Nemo won't stay lost for long.

Hands-on fun

After a quick look at the aquarium, you enter an area called Sea Base. This is your chance to take a closer look at the creatures and to try out the hands-on exhibits. Be sure to visit the Nemo and Friends room, where you can find a real-life version of the little guy. Younger kids get a kick out of Bruce's Shark World. (It's a cool play area where you can learn about sharks.)

Talk to the turtle

Everyone seems to love Turtle Talk with Crush. It's a show that lets you talk to the cartoon critter. The best part? He talks back. It is totally awesome, dude!

THE LAND

The building called The Land looks like a big greenhouse. Some of its attractions focus on food and where it comes from. There's a boat ride and a movie about the environment. It stars Simba, Timon, and Pumbaa from *The Lion King*. Soarin' is another ride here. It lets guests fly high in the sky.

Hidden Mickey Alert!

Study the paintings while you wait in line for Living with the Land. One has bubbles on it that connect to form a Mickey head.

PHOTO BY JILL SAFRO

Living with the Land

What's the most popular fruit on our planet? The banana! People eat more bananas than any other fruity snack. You'll learn lots more food facts on this boat trip. The boat travels through rooms that look like a rain forest, a desert, and a prairie. Then it heads to a modern greenhouse area.

A recording explains all the things your boat floats past. If you are lucky, you will see some giant vegetables growing here. The greenhouse has produced some of the biggest lemons and eggplants in the world.

In all, The Land grows more than 30 tons of fruit and veggies each year. A lot of it is served to guests in Epcot restaurants like the Garden Grill and Coral Reef.

The Reader Review

A Great Big Beautiful Day!

By: Sean, age 8
Schenectady, NY

I thought this ride was fun, and it taught me a lot about nature. I especially liked visiting the greenhouse. It was neat to see all sorts of plants from all around the world growing under one roof.

Hidden Mickey Alert!
Look up in the cloud under the blue balloon at The Land pavilion's center.

The Circle of Life

Simba, Timon, and Pumbaa are together again. This time they're in a movie about the importance of protecting the Earth's environment. The film is a mix of animation and live action. It shows some of the problems we face — and how we can try to fix them.

Timber!

The movie's opening scene shows animals just like those in *The Lion King* (but these animals are real). Next, you see Simba near a watering hole. All of a sudden he hears "Timber!" and is drenched by the splash of a tree falling into water. Timon and Pumbaa are clearing the grassland to build a resort (the Hakuna Matata Lakeside Village).

Simba tells a story

Simba remembers what his father taught him about the importance of caring for the land. He tells Timon and Pumbaa a story about how humans sometimes forget that everything is connected in the great Circle of Life.

The Reader Review
A Great Big Beautiful Day!

By: Luke, age 9
Fairview, PA

I really enjoyed the Circle of Life film. In it, everyone works together to clean up the environment. It makes you feel like you can make a difference by taking care of the world. Little kids might be bored by this movie.

Soarin'

Have you ever wondered what it's like to be a bird? To swoop and soar high above the ground and way up into the clouds? This attraction lets you experience that first-hand.

Fasten your safety belt

Before the fun starts, you will grab a seat in one of the hang gliders. Put your stuff in the basket, fasten your seat belt, sit back, and get ready.

Up, up, and away!

As your glider lifts off the ground, a giant movie screen lights up in front of you. On it, you will see many scenes from the state of California. During the journey, flyers glide past Yosemite Valley, the Golden Gate Bridge, and the desert in Death Valley.

Many scenes were filmed using special cameras on airplanes and helicopters. Your glider moves the way those aircraft did — so it feels like you are really flying.

How real does it feel? Some people lift their feet when they fly over the forest — because it seems like their toes will hit the treetops! At one point, it even smells real (an orange grove smells like oranges)!

The whole trip takes about five minutes. You must be at least 40 inches tall to ride. If you get motion sickness or are afraid of heights, skip this one!

The Reader Review

By: Isobel, age 10
Traverse City, MI

In Soarin', you do just that — you SOAR up in the air! You also tilt and lean just like you are flying. I really like how calm and relaxing this ride is.

INNOVENTIONS

Innoventions is all about hands-on fun. Here, exhibits showcase imaginative products and invite you to try them out. You become a product safety tester or a firefighter for the day, or jump inside a video game. And don't miss The Sum of All Thrills. This special ride lets you design and ride your own roller coaster!

There are two buildings (called Innoventions East and Innoventions West) filled with lots of stuff to explore. The exhibits are always changing — so even if you have been here before, it is worth a peek. If you visit at night, check out the sidewalks in Innoventions Plaza: They light up!

The Reader Review

By: Dylan, age 16
Mt. Pleasant, SC

The best part of Innoventions is The Sum of All Thrills. It is so much fun to design your own roller coaster and then feel what it would be like to ride it!

IMAGINATION!

This pavilion is like a workout for your imagination — the attractions really make you think! There is an interesting ride that tests your creativity, a hands-on activity center, and a musical 3-D movie called *Captain EO*. Outside, the jumping waters of the Leap Frog Fountains are sure to cool you off and keep you guessing. There are a lot of other ways to have fun here, too. Just use your imagination!

HOT TiP!

On a hot day, cool off by trying to catch the streams of water that jump from fountain to fountain at the entertaining Leap Frog Fountains.

ImageWorks

Once you get inside ImageWorks, it may be hard to leave. Young kids love it because it has hands-on (and feet-on) activities. And now it's even better, because there are a few new things to see and do.

Most kids agree that one of their favorite stops is the electric philharmonic. In it, you can use your hands to make music and conduct

a virtual orchestra. How? Simply wave them about or move them up and down — it's that easy! And there's more, so plan to spend about 20 minutes here. (One activity lets you send a creative e-mail message, so be sure to have your address handy!) There is a small shop inside, too. New activities may be added, so even if you've been here before, it is worth another visit.

Journey Into Imagination with Figment

Think how different the world would be without any imagination in it. There would be no stories to tell, no pictures to draw, and no inventions to make things easier. One thing is for sure — Walt Disney World would not exist! Imagination is so important to the folks at Disney that they made a special place in Future World to learn all about it.

It's called the Imagination Institute — and it's having an open house. That means everyone is invited to learn about all of its projects. And who better to take you on a tour of this special place than Figment himself? (Figment is a little purple dragon. He hosts this attraction. That's him in the picture. A lot of kids are Figment fans.)

Epcot

Epcot Character Spot

Sure, there are lots of places to meet characters at Epcot. But do you want to know where the best place is? It is inside Innoventions West and it is chock-full of Disney characters!

Of course, this is Epcot, so the characters greet you in specially themed areas. The themes? Transportation, space, energy, land, and communication. If they sound familiar, it is because those are some of the themes that are featured in Future World.

The characters take turns greeting guests throughout the day. Expect to find Disney pals like Mickey Mouse, Minnie Mouse, Goofy, Chip, and Dale. Of course, you never know who else might show up — so keep those cameras and the autograph section of this book handy.

Captain EO

Ready for a thrilling space adventure? Head straight for the Captain EO theater. This 3-D movie has something for everyone — cuddly critters, awesome aliens, a nasty villain, and a bit of magic.

Some special effects add to the excitement. And, thanks to special 3-D glasses, the action on the screen seems quite real.

The action follows Captain EO (played by Michael Jackson) on a musical journey to outer space. It gets a little scary at times —

especially when EO meets the evil leader of a dark planet. But don't worry — it all ends happily.

Most older kids enjoy this 17-minute, 3-D experience.

The Reader Review

By: Garrison, age 12
West Bend, WI

Captain Eo is a very cool show. The star, Michael Jackson, and his crew go to a distant planet. It has awesome music. It's great fun!

HOT TIP

If your hair is long, put it in a ponytail before riding Test Track, or it might get all tangled up.

Reader Tip

"If you need to cool off, be sure to visit Cool Wash (it's near Test Track). It looks like a car wash, but it's for people. You'll be sprayed with a nice cool mist."

Katie (age 12)
Palatine Bridge, NY

Disney's FASTPASS

TEST TRACK

WILD · SCARY · LOUD
Attraction Reaction

READER #6 RIDE PLEASER

What is it like to design and test a new car? Find out in this thrilling ride — and learn what it's like to make a cool, safe car.

Where are the brakes?

Test Track is one of Walt Disney World's fastest rides and Epcot's original thrill ride. After you design a car on a touch screen, you can test it on the track. Your car has no steering wheel or brake pedals for you to control, but its sound and video equipment let you know what's being tested. You zip around curves, zoom down a street, and bounce on bumpy roads. At one point, you nearly crash into a truck!

A crash course in car safety

Kids think this ride is a fun way to learn more about cars. Parts of it are loud, so don't be startled if you hear a crash. And don't worry — the ride is safer than it looks. Disney workers tested the cars first. After all, that's what test-driving is all about.

You must be at least 40 inches tall to try it.

After the ride, check out the post-show area. It's pretty cool.

THIS IS YOUR VEHICLE!

PHOTO BY MIKE CARROLL

Epcot

The Reader Review

A Great Big Beautiful Day!

By: Eric, age 12
Beverly Hills, CA

Test Track is the fastest, most surprising ride I have ever been on. I learned about car testing while having fun. I thought I would be scared, but I really enjoyed myself.

PHOTO BY JILL SAFRO

LOUD
Attraction Reaction

DARK
Attraction Reaction

Reader Tip

"Try to sit in the front left car. That way you'll be the first to go through the ride!" (If you can't, don't worry — all the seats have good views.)

Danny (age 12)
Springfield, IL

UNIVERSE OF ENERGY

Discover where energy comes from on this trip through prehistoric times, complete with dinosaurs. The ride is called Ellen's Energy Adventure. It is inside the Universe of Energy pavilion. Ellen may be familiar to you — she is TV's Ellen DeGeneres.

Ellen's energy nightmare

The attraction starts with a movie about Ellen. She is asleep and having a weird dream. In it, she's a contestant on a game show and all of the questions are about energy. Ellen doesn't know much about energy, so she stinks at the game.

Then Bill Nye the Science Guy decides to teach her all about energy. To do it, he takes her (and you) on a trip back in time.

Visit the dinosaurs

First you go into a theater to see another movie. Then the ride part begins. Bill Nye takes you and Ellen to a prehistoric world. You travel through fog and past several different types of dinosaurs. Some of them are huge. And they all look real. Be careful or one might sneeze on you.

At the end of the ride, Ellen gets another chance to play on the game show. How does she do this time? That's something you'll have to see for yourself!

Three cheers for energy!

Some kids like this ride because it's a fun way to learn about energy. But others enjoy it for the dinosaurs. This attraction only operates during very busy times of the year and may not be open during your visit.

The Reader Review A Great Big Beautiful Day!

By: Nicholas, age 10
Vancouver, WA

This show is funny and teaches you a lot about where energy comes from. My favorite part is when the theater seats turn into ride cars and start to move!

World Showcase

Anybody can be a world traveler — or a secret agent — at World Showcase. You can learn about other countries, experience different cultures, and meet people from all over the world. You can also be a super spy and save the world in an interactive adventure (see page 72 for details).

As you visit each of the countries, be sure to talk to the folks who work there. Most of the people in each pavilion really come from the country they represent. The pavilions were built around a lake called World Showcase Lagoon. If you make the trip all the way around the lake, you will walk more than one mile!

(see page 72 for details).

Hidden Mickey Alert!

The iron grates that the trees in World Showcase grow out of could probably tell a mouse tale or two. They're covered with Hidden Mickeys!

Reader Tip

"If you want to learn more about some of the pavilions in Epcot, stop at Guest Relations. They have lots of interesting fact sheets."

Benjamin (age 11)
Geneseo, NY

Epcot

CANADA

If you look at a map of North America, Canada is at the top, just above the United States. It is a beautiful country. The Canada pavilion at Epcot is very pretty, too. There's a rocky mountain, a stream, gardens, and a totem pole.

The highlight is a movie called *O Canada!* The scenes completely surround you. Since you stand the whole time, it's easy to turn around and see everything. Many kids enjoy the movie but wish the theater had seats.

The Reader Review

By: Shelby, age 14
Calgary, Alberta, Canada

This pavilion shows what Canadians are proud of. I should know — I'm from Canada! I wish the film included even more, but it's a great introduction to my country.

UNITED KINGDOM

From London to the English countryside, this pavilion gives a varied view of the United Kingdom. Some details to look for include the smoke stains painted on the chimneys to make them appear old, and the grassy roofs that are really made of plastic broom bristles.

The Reader Review

By: Cody, age 9
Staten Island, NY

Take a picture by the red telephone booths like the ones in England. Also, see if the band is playing in the garden. Older kids and adults will like to hear them play.

International Mouse

Mickey Mouse is famous all over the world. But not everyone knows the movie-star mouse by that name. In Italy he's called Topolino. In Greece he's known as Miky Maoye. Norwegians call him Mikke Mus. In Sweden he goes by Musse Pigg. And in China he's Mi Lao Shu. That's a lot of names for one mouse to remember!

FRANCE

The Eiffel Tower is probably the best-known landmark at the France pavilion. (The real one is in Paris, France.) The buildings here look just like those in a real French town. Many of the workers here come from France. They speak English with a French accent. Surprise them by saying *bonjour* (pronounced: *bohn-zhoor*). It means "good day" in French.

The main attraction — besides the treats at the bakery — is Impressions de France (that means Impressions of France). It's a movie that takes you from one end of France to the other. It's shown on a big screen, and you get to sit down and take in the sights.

The Reader Review

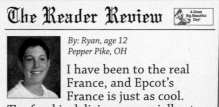

By: Ryan, age 12
Pepper Pike, OH

I have been to the real France, and Epcot's France is just as cool. The food is delicious, especially at the bakery. I think everyone will enjoy the entertainment, shops, and food.

Topiary Trees

PHOTO BY JILL SAFRO

There's something unusual about some of the trees and shrubs growing at Walt Disney World — they're shaped like animals! Some look like Disney characters. These plants are called topiaries (pronounced: *TOE-pea-air-eez*). They are carefully trimmed by gardeners to keep their exact form. You may spot an Alice topiary by the Mad Tea Party in the Magic Kingdom and a Mary Poppins tree at the Grand Floridian resort. Disney World has more than 200 topiaries in all. How many can you find?

HOT TiP!

Don't miss the special entertainment in each of the countries.

MOROCCO

The country of Morocco is famous for its mosaics — artwork and patterns that are made up of many tiles. That's why there is such beautiful tile work on the walls of this pavilion. Moroccan artists made sure the mosaics here were done right.

The buildings are copies of monuments in Moroccan cities, including Fez and Marrakesh. There are many shops selling items you could find in Morocco. You can buy baskets, brass, jewelry, sandals, a fez (a type of hat), and other Moroccan clothing.

A belly dancer entertains guests at the Marrakesh restaurant. And a band called Mo'Rockin performs in the courtyard.

Salaam alaikum (pronounced: *sah-LAHM wah-LAY-koom*) means "hello" in Morocco. (It's Arabic.)

Epcot

PHOTO BY JILL SAFRO

Reader Tip

"Try to eat meals early or late in the day to avoid long lines!"

John (age 14)
Washington Township, NJ

JAPAN

The giant temple out front, called a pagoda, makes the Japanese pavilion easy to spot. It's modeled after a famous pagoda in the city of Nara, Japan.

Be sure to notice all of the evergreen trees. In Japan, they are symbols of eternal life. Some of the trees found in a traditional Japanese garden will not survive in Florida. Similar trees were used instead.

Japanese drummers often perform outside the pavilion. The huge department store has lots of souvenirs from Japan. Want to say "good morning" in Japanese? Just say *ohayo gozaimasu* (pronounced: *oh-hi-yoh goh-zy-ee-mahs*).

Just for Kids!

Epcot has something special for younger kids: Kidcot Fun Stops. There's one in each of the countries of World Showcase. At each of these spots, you can use crayons to color cutouts of Duffy the Disney Bear, make crafts, and learn how kids have fun in countries all over the world.

THE AMERICAN ADVENTURE

The United States of America is the star of this pavilion. That's why it's called the American Adventure.

The American Adventure show takes place inside a building that looks a bit like Independence Hall (the real Independence Hall is in Philadelphia, Pennsylvania). The show celebrates the American spirit throughout U.S. history.

Benjamin Franklin and Mark Twain host the show. They look so real, you may forget that they are mechanical. Ben Franklin even walks up stairs!

The American Adventure show honors many heroes from history: the pilgrims, Alexander Graham Bell, Jackie Robinson, Susan B. Anthony, Walt Disney, and others. It's a great way to learn about American history. It's best for older kids.

The Reader Review

A Great Big Beautiful Day!

By: Joshua, age 12
Cheektowaga, NY

The American Adventure is educational yet entertaining. It is impossible to leave without a smile on your face and a true feeling of pride for being an American.

Hidden Mickey Alert!

Let your eyes follow the fireworks that burst from behind the Statue of Liberty. One of them leaves a Mickey-shaped puff of smoke (in the American Adventure attraction).

ITALY

Venice is an Italian city known for waterways called canals. There are no canals at Epcot's Italy, but the pavilion does look a lot like the real thing. The tower is a smaller version of the Campanile, a famous building in Venice.

Notice the gondolas (pronounced: *GAHN-doe-lahz*) tied to the dock in the lagoon. They are a type of boat used for traveling in the canals of Venice.

Say *buon giorno* (pronounced: *bwon JOR-no*). It means "good day" in Italian.

GERMANY

Hidden Mickey Alert!
You'll find a Mickey in the grass in Germany's miniature village.

There isn't a village in Germany quite like the one at Epcot. It's a combination of cities and small towns from all around the country. Try to stop by the pavilion on the hour so you can see the special cuckoo clock near the toy shop and hear it chime.

In German, "good day" is *guten tag* (say: *GOO-ten tahg*).

The Reader Review

By: Micheline, age 9
Coral Springs, FL

Germany is one of my favorite pavilions. I love the cuckoo clocks, teddy bears, and sausages! A great time to visit Germany is in October for Oktoberfest. There are special games, food, singing, and dancing.

CHINA

Disney's version of the Temple of Heaven is at the center of this pavilion. It's a landmark in the Chinese city of Beijing. Inside, there is a Circle-Vision 360 movie called *Reflections of China*. (There are no seats in the theater.)

Before going in to see the movie, take a look at the waiting area. It's decorated in shades of red and gold. These colors mean good luck in China.

The film takes guests on a tour of the country. It's worth seeing, but it is more popular with adults than kids. Most kids would rather spend their time checking out the fish in the koi pond or listening to the flute

PHOTO BY JILL SAFRO

The Reader Review

By: Beckie, age 9
Gettysburg, PA

I really like China. It's got massive gift shops, a pond with fish, and lots of food, plus a movie! I could spend a year — and a lot of money — here.

music performed in the courtyard.

To say "hello" in Chinese, say *ni hao* (pronounced: *nee HOW*).

Hidden Mickey Alert!
Look in the mural above the line for a Viking wearing Mickey Mouse ears.

FASTPASS

Reader Tip

"Sit in the back of the boat on Maelstrom for the best view."
Sam (age 15)
San Diego, CA

NORWAY

DARK
Attraction Reaction

SCARY
Attraction Reaction

You will discover the history and culture of Norway at this pavilion. (Don't worry about the angry, three-headed troll. He's harmless.)

The main building is a castle. It was based on an ancient fortress in the capital city of Oslo. Inside, there is a ride called Maelstrom. It's about Norway's history.

The ride begins in a Viking village. (Vikings were explorers who lived about 1,000 years ago. Many came from Norway.) Next you travel to a forest, where a three-headed troll curses your boat and makes it go backward. After the boat trip, there is a short movie about Norway.

Saying "hello" is easy here. It's *god dag* (say: *goo DAHG*).

The Reader Review

A Great Big Beautiful Day!

By: Derek, age 9
Grayslake, IL

I liked this ride a lot, but I could have skipped the movie after it. My favorite part was when the troll curses your boat and you almost fall backward over a waterfall!

Phineas and Ferb: Agent P's World Showcase Adventure

How would you like to become a secret agent and help Perry the Platypus fight evil scientist Dr. Heinz Doofenshmirtz? Here's your chance! The interactive game is based on the Disney Channel show *Phineas and Ferb*. Of course, you don't have to know the show to have fun playing along here. Once you borrow a F.O.N.E. (which stands for Field Operative Notification Equipment) from a recruitment station, you are ready to start the hunt for clues. Check a park guidemap for pick-up locations.

If you follow instructions and find the clues, you will complete your very important mission: to save the world! There is no charge to play, but you do need to return the F.O.N.E. when you're done. Grown-ups love this, too — so invite your parents to play along! This game replaced the Kim Possible Adventure.

Hidden Mickey Alert!

The volcano at the beginning of the boat ride is about to erupt! Watch the swirling smoke carefully and you might spot that famous mouse.

MEXICO

The pyramid-shaped building at the Mexico pavilion is home to an attraction called Gran Fiesta Tour Starring the Three Caballeros. It is a boat trip that takes you through the country of Mexico.

The Three Caballeros are José, Panchito, and Donald (Duck, that is). They starred in a movie together way back in 1944. Now they're back together and planning to do a big show in Mexico City. But there is a problem. Donald keeps getting lost! Don't worry, there is a happy ending. This is Disney World, after all. "Hello" here is *hola* (say: *OH-lah*).

The Reader Review

By: Jason, age 9
Interlachen, FL

I was disappointed to learn El Rio Del Tiempo was replaced by this ride, but I'm happy they left most of the best parts and added a lot of fun. It's great for the whole family.

Entertainment

Epcot is known for its awesome entertainment. There are lots of shows and special performances every day of the year. For more information, check a park Times Guide.

ILLUMINATIONS — REFLECTIONS OF EARTH

An amazing fireworks show takes place each night on and around World Showcase Lagoon. It tells the story of Earth's history. You can get a good view of it from anywhere around the lagoon.

The Reader Review

A Great Big Beautiful Day!

By: Jordan, age 14
Maynard, MA

IllumiNations is absolutely beautiful. It's a great way of telling the story of Earth's creation. You can get a good view from anywhere around the lagoon, but I like to watch from the United Kingdom.

JAMMITORS

One of the loudest and wildest shows is inside Future World, where musicians bang out rhythms on trash cans and, sometimes, on one another.

WORLD SHOWCASE PERFORMERS

There is some form of entertainment at each of the pavilions in World Showcase. Some of the highlights include acrobats in France, the Voices of Liberty at the American Adventure, drummers in Japan, a juggler in Italy, and a Canadian rock band known as Off-Kilter. The Voices of Liberty sing patriotic songs. Feel free to sing along.

Where to find

Characters

at EPCOT

The best place to meet characters is at the **Epcot Character Spot** in **Innoventions West** in Future World (page 59). Different characters take turns hanging out there, so you never know who you might see. One thing you can be sure of: They will always be happy to sign autographs and pose for pictures.

You may also run into characters from classic Disney films while wandering around **World Showcase**. They usually show up during the afternoon hours. Don't forget to ask the characters to sign the autograph section of this book.

Epcot

Start your day early at Soarin', followed by Test Track, and the "less intense" version of Mission SPACE. Then stop in to say hi to Nemo at The Seas with Nemo and Friends. After that, head over to the Imagination pavilion.

Remember: World Showcase doesn't open until 11 A.M.

Need a refreshing splash? Visit Cool Wash by Test Track, the squirting sidewalk that leads to World Showcase, or the fountain by Mission SPACE.

Check the electronic Tip Board in Innoventions Plaza. It lets you know how long the wait is for many attractions.

Each World Showcase country has its own special stamp. Visit the Kidcot Funstop in each place and you can collect all the stamps on the last pages of this book!

Innoventions is very big and can be tiring. Visit it early in the day or after a meal, when you are rested and full of energy.

Bring Disney pins with you so you'll have something to trade with guests at the pin-trading booth in Future World. (Get a parent's permission before you trade anything.)

Try not to squeeze the movies at Canada, France, and China all into one day.

Take time to talk to the people who work in World Showcase. Most of them come from the country of the pavilion they represent, and they have many interesting stories to tell.

You can sample soda for free at Club Cool. It's in Future World (near Innoventions).

Attraction Ratings

REALLY COOL
(Don't Miss)

- The American Adventure
- Journey Into Imagination with Figment
- Innoventions
- Gran Fiesta Tour
- France
- Canada
- Living with the Land
- Mexico
- ImageWorks

THE COOLEST
(See at Least Twice)

- Test Track
- Universe of Energy
- Captain EO
- Norway
- Spaceship Earth
- Mission SPACE
- Soarin'
- The Seas with Nemo and Friends
- IllumiNations

COOL
(Check It Out)

- The Circle of Life movie in The Land
- China
- Italy
- United Kingdom
- Morocco
- Germany
- Japan

Your favorite Epcot attractions

_____

_____

_____

_____

_____

Disney's Hollywood Studios

Disney's Hollywood Studios lets you learn about some of the magic of making movies and TV shows. There are attractions that show how animation is done, how special effects are created, how stunts are performed, and lots more.

The Studios looks a little like Hollywood did back in the 1940s. Hollywood is the California city where movie-making got its big start. Disney's Hollywood Studios got its big start in 1989. It has attractions based on *Toy Story*, *The Little Mermaid*, *The Muppets*, *Star Wars*, and other favorites.

One of the best things about this park is that you can be a part of some attractions. It's fun to be right in the middle of the action, so be sure to volunteer. You will also get to meet a ton of characters, including the stars of some of Disney's recent animated hits — remember to bring a pen for their autographs.

Use this map to explore Disney's Hollywood Studios theme park.

A **Beauty and the Beast — Live on Stage**

B **Fantasmic!**

C **The Twilight Zone Tower of Terror**

D **Rock 'n' Roll Roller Coaster**

E **The Magic of Disney Animation**

F **Disney Jr. — Live on Stage!**

G **Walt Disney: One Man's Dream**

H **Voyage of The Little Mermaid**

I **Toy Story Mania!**

J **Studio Backlot Tour**

K **American Film Institute Showcase**

L **Honey, I Shrunk the Kids Movie Set Adventure**

M **Muppet★Vision 3-D**

N **Star Tours — The Adventures Continue**

O **Indiana Jones Epic Stunt Spectacular**

P **The American Idol® Experience**

Q **The Great Movie Ride**

R **Lights, Motors, Action! Extreme Stunt Show**

Pixar Place

Hollywood Blvd.

Sunset Blvd.

Streets of America

Disney's Hollywood Studios

▶Bus Transportation

Walt Disney World Resort Guest Boat Transportation ▶

HOT TiP!

If you need something to hold on to while riding Tower, grab the handle beside your seat.

SCARY Attraction Reaction

WILD Attraction Reaction

DARK Attraction Reaction

The Twilight Zone™ Tower of Terror

Disney's FASTPASS

At a height of 199 feet, Tower of Terror is one of the tallest attractions at Walt Disney World. For some people, it's also the scariest.

Legend says that one Halloween night, lightning hit The Hollywood Tower Hotel. A whole section of the hotel disappeared! So did an elevator carrying five people. No one ever saw them again.

Haunted hotel

Now the hotel is haunted. If you dare to enter it, you are in for a few surprises. First, you walk through the dusty hotel lobby. Then you enter a tiny room, where Rod Serling appears on TV. (He was the host of a show called *The Twilight Zone*.) Once Rod tells you the story of The Hollywood Tower Hotel, get ready — you are on your way to the Twilight Zone.

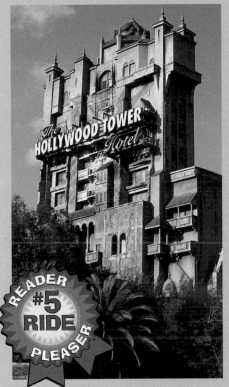

READER #5 RIDE PLEASER

Going down!

After waiting in the boiler room for a bit, you are given a seat in a big elevator. The elevator takes you on a short tour of the hotel, where you see some special effects. But the highlight comes when the elevator cables snap. *Whoosh!* You plunge eight stories! Next, the elevator shoots up to the hotel's 13th floor. It teeters for a moment and then . . . it drops again and again at blazing speed! You must be at least 40 inches tall to ride.

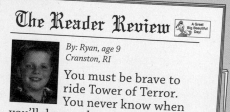

The Reader Review

A Great Big Beautiful Day!

By: Ryan, age 9
Cranston, RI

You must be brave to ride Tower of Terror. You never know when you'll drop or how many times the elevator will go up and down. It is suspense to the max!

Rock 'n' Roller Coaster Starring Aerosmith

This ride rocks! It travels at top speed and flips you upside down three times. It also has a rock 'n' roll soundtrack that will have you dancing in your seat.

You're invited

Rock 'n' Roller Coaster goes really fast — it takes you from zero to 60 miles per hour in the first three seconds of the ride! You need the speed because you're on your way to a party at an Aerosmith concert — and you're running late.

It's showtime!

The ride takes place in a stretch limousine on a roller coaster track. The limousine's radio is tuned to the concert. You can hear the band warming up, but your car is not moving yet. Then, just as the concert starts, the light turns green and you're on your way. You zoom along the California highway and make it just in time for the end of the show. Hang on!

You must be at least 48 inches tall to ride Rock 'n' Roller Coaster.

The Reader Review

By: Kate, age 13
Sewell, NJ

Woo-hoo! This is the best roller coaster in all of Disney World. I like it because it goes really fast and I like the music.

Beauty and the Beast — Live on Stage

It's hard to keep quiet during this stage show — it makes you want to clap and sing along. The music comes straight from Disney's animated film *Beauty and the Beast*.

As the show begins, Belle is frustrated by life in her small town. She is dreaming of exciting, faraway places. Later on, she becomes a prisoner in the Beast's castle. All of the castle's residents are under a

magic spell! Lumiere, Cogsworth, Mrs. Potts, and the rest of the gang are there to help Belle (and perform "Be Our Guest"). In the end, the spell is broken. The Beast becomes human again.

The show is performed several times a day. Read a park Times Guide for schedules and dates. You can get a free Times Guide in many shops in the park. Just ask.

The Reader Review

A Great Big Beautiful Day!

By: Pharra, age 11
Alpharetta, GA

I liked the lively colors and the music in this show. I didn't like how it skipped so fast from one song to the next, because that made it more challenging to follow along, but I still got the story. It's a show the entire family can enjoy!

Disney's Hollywood Studios

81

HOT TiP!

The sidewalk by The Great Movie Ride is covered with handprints and footprints. They belong to famous performers. Put your palms and feet in the prints and compare yours with the stars'. (Wash your hands when you are done.)

Hidden Mickey Alert!

Mickey and pals are drawn on the Well of Souls. Look for them on the wall during the Indiana Jones scene.

FASTPASS

DARK
Attraction Reaction

SCARY
Attraction Reaction

The Great Movie Ride

How many movies have you seen in your lifetime? Hundreds? Thousands? Well, how many have you actually been in? Probably not too many! This attraction lets you ride through scenes from several old movies.

Pay attention!

First, you'll watch short clips from famous films. Pay close attention — these are the scenes that you will visit later on.

As you enter the ride vehicle, take time to look around. The room is set up like a movie set (a stage where movie scenes are filmed). The background looks like the hills of Hollywood. That's the California town where movie-making got its big start.

A trip to Munchkinland

Once the car starts moving, you'll pass through scenes from movies like *Mary Poppins*, *Alien*, and *Fantasia*. One of the best scenes is straight out of *The Wizard of Oz*. It looks just like Munchkinland! (Beware: The Wicked Witch of the West pops in for a visit.)

The Reader Review
A Great Big Beautiful Day!

By: Philip, age 12
Glen Carbon, IL

I am not really a fan of old movies, but I loved this ride. I felt like I was in the movie scenes. The best part was when the tour guide got kidnapped. I sat by my grandma, and since she loves movies, this ride was a big hit for her, too!

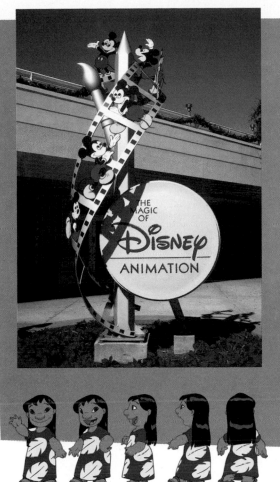

The Magic of Disney Animation

Anybody can create a cartoon character. All you need is a pencil, some paper, and a little imagination. But how do you get that character to *move*? That's where the animation part comes in.

This attraction shows you how *Tarzan*, *Lilo and Stitch*, and other animated movies were made. In the waiting area there are drawings on the walls. Later, you'll find out how artists called *animators* bring these kinds of sketches to life.

The Reader Review

By: Nicholas, age 9
Winston-Salem, NC

This attraction is very cool. I like the funny movie at the beginning. And I love the machine that asks you questions and decides which Disney character you are most like. I'm like Cogsworth.

Disney's Hollywood Studios

Who am I?

- I live in Arendelle.
- Flowers make me sneeze.
- I like warm hugs!

Answer: Olaf

Hidden Mickey Alert!
Lasers at the start of the show form a Mickey head.

PHOTO BY JILL SAFRO

The Reader Review A Great Big Beautiful Day!

By: Jessica, age 12
Williamsville, NY

If you're a *Little Mermaid* fan, this attraction is a "must"! The only bad part? The seats are low. Try not to sit behind people who are very tall.

SCARY
Attraction Reaction

LOUD
Attraction Reaction

DARK
Attraction Reaction

Voyage of The Little Mermaid

DISNEY'S FASTPASS

You don't have to be a fish to have fun underwater — and this show proves it. In it, you go below the ocean's surface with Ariel and her friends from *The Little Mermaid*. They sing and act out the story on a stage. Ariel and Eric star along with puppets, including Flounder, Sebastian, and other sea creatures.

Under the sea

There are some great special effects that draw you into the show. A screen of water makes it seem like the theater really is under the sea. Lasers flash, lightning strikes, and mist sprays the audience. Scenes from the movie are shown on a big screen behind the stage.

A winning combination

The combination of people, puppets, and special effects makes for a terrific show. To get the best view of all the action, try sitting toward the back of the theater. From there, the puppets look like they are really swimming!

Disney Junior — Live on Stage!

Are you a Disney Junior fan? If so, head straight to this attraction. Friends from Disney Junior programs will dazzle you in a colorful stage show. Expect to find characters from *Mickey Mouse Clubhouse, Doc McStuffins, Sofia the First, Jake and the Never Land Pirates*, and more.

Have a seat on the floor!

When you walk into the theater, you will notice something unusual about it — there are no seats. But don't worry. The carpet is quite comfy, so sit down and make yourself at home. (There are a few benches in the back. Grown-ups like to sit on them.)

A big hit with little guests

Big kids may get a kick out of Disney Junior — Live on Stage!, but little kids seem to have the most fun here. If you have younger brothers or sisters, be sure to bring them to this show.

The Reader Review

A Great Big Beautiful Day!

By: Hannah, age 14
Scotia, NY

It is nice to see how much fun young kids have when they see their favorite characters from Disney Junior. This is a good show to see with your little brother or sister. It is fun to sing and dance along with the characters!

HOT TiP!
This show is very popular with young kids. Check show times and be sure to arrive early.

Disney's Hollywood Studios

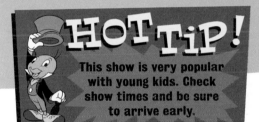

Who am I?

- My last name is Davis.
- Molly is my little sister.
- My room is full of toys.

Answer: Andy

Lights, Motors, Action!
Extreme Stunt Show

High-speed car chases, loud crashes, and giant splashes happen in lots of movies and TV shows. Of course, they are all staged by experts who fool you into thinking all the action is real and sometimes dangerous. This stunt show has all of the above, plus a whole lot more in-your-face action. It gives guests a behind the scenes look at how the folks in Hollywood make amazing stunts seem so realistic.

Many kids think this is a very exciting show. But it can be a little scary, too — especially when it seems like a stunt person is on fire. Don't worry, it's all part of the show — the performer is wearing a protective suit. If you don't like fire or loud noises, sit in the back of the theater. It's less intense back there.

The Reader Review

By: Abagail, age 11
Sequim, WA

I want to watch this show over and over. It explains how action scenes are made in movies. The cars go really fast and some go backwards. It's amazing!

PHOTO BY JILL SAFRO

Hidden Mickey Alert!

He is in the rocks by the exit. This one is hard to find!

PHOTO BY JILL SAFRO

Reader Tip

"Ponchos aren't just handy when it rains. They're great for rides that get you wet, too!"

Amy (age 11)
New Castle, PA

Studio Backlot Tour

SCARY
Attraction Reaction

LOUD
Attraction Reaction

There used to be a working film studio inside this theme park. A tram ride lets you see parts of the backstage areas where movies and TV shows were made. You also get an inside peek at the secrets behind some special effects.

Very special effects

The first stop on the tour is beside a big pool of water. There's a little boat and a human host. Your host shows you how film-makers can take a sunny theme park day and turn it into a dark, stormy day at sea. You'll also learn how a toy battle can seem real with a little bit of movie-making know-how.

A grand canyon

The trip includes a stop at Catastrophe Canyon — a special effects area. Here you see a fire and a flash flood. (You may get a little bit wet.) The tram also takes you through the costume department and past props from famous movies.

The Reader Review

By: Abby, age 10
Pepper Pike, OH

The tour is good for people who want to learn about movie-making. It's sort of slow, so if you are in the mood for speedy stuff, it is not for you.

Reader Tip

"Before you go to a theme park, decide on your number one must-see and get a Fastpass for it."

Jessilyn (age 13)
Billings, MT

Honey, I Shrunk the Kids Movie Set Adventure

The backyard from the *Honey, I Shrunk the Kids* movie has been re-created as a big playground. Even grown-ups feel small here. There are 30-foot blades of grass, a giant toy truck, and much more. There are things to climb on, slide down, and explore.

Most kids enjoy getting wet under the leaky garden hose. Nobody stays dry!

It's a great way to cool off after all that running and climbing.

The Reader Review A Great Big Beautiful Day!

By: Marcelo, age 6
Coral Gables, FL

You feel as small as an ant in this giant backyard. And there's so much to do! There's a huge spiderweb to climb and tree roots that you can step on to make music. It's lots of fun!

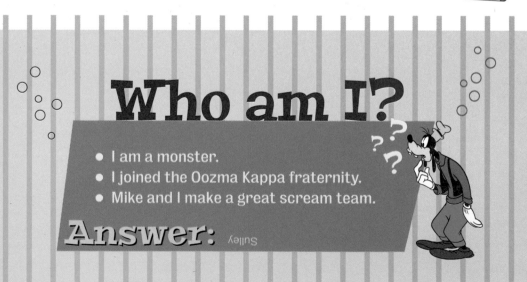

Who am I?

- I am a monster.
- I joined the Oozma Kappa fraternity.
- Mike and I make a great scream team.

Answer: Sulley

Hidden Mickey Alert!

The Muppets have made some Hidden Mickeys of their own! Look on their building for funny eyes and noses that together form the shape of Mickey heads.

Reader Tip

"Don't rush to be the first one in the theater — you'll have to sit at the end of your row and the view is better from the middle."

David (age 14)
Calabasas, CA

Disney's FASTPASS

Muppet★Vision 3-D

Don't miss this attraction — it's one of Walt Disney World's best. It begins with a funny pre-show starring Fozzie Bear, Gonzo, Scooter, and Sam Eagle. Then you go into a special theater that looks just like the one from Jim Henson's *The Muppet Show*. Here, you see 3-D movie effects mixed with some other special tricks.

Amazing effects

Some of the effects are so good that it's hard to tell what's part of the movie and what's real. During Miss Piggy's big song, bubbles look like they are just inches away from you. Don't be surprised if they really are.

Look around the theater

Be sure to look all around you when you're watching the show. Some of the best action happens off the screen. Try to keep an eye out for the Swedish Chef. He is cooking up a plan in the back of the theater.

The Reader Review — *A Great Big Beautiful Day!*

By: Carrie, age 13
Hinsdale, IL

This is an all-around great show. I recommend it to everyone! The characters in the movie come right out at you, and you feel like you could reach out and touch them. It's very cool!

Reader Tip

"Star Tours really pulls you around and shakes you up. Be prepared for a wild ride!"

Kinsey (age 7)
Athens, GA

Who am I?

- I work very hard.
- I believe in wishes.
- My shoes are made of glass.

Answer: Cinderella

HOT TiP!

There are about 50 different versions of Star Tours, so each adventure is a surprise!

WILD — Attraction Reaction

LOUD — Attraction Reaction

SCARY — Attraction Reaction

Star Tours — The Adventures Continue

DISNEY'S FASTPASS

If you've ever been to Star Tours before, you should come back soon — it's a little different almost every time. The journey through the galaxy makes guests feel like they are part of a *Star Wars* movie. Before the trip starts, be sure to put on the special glasses — this adventure is in 3-D. Keep your eye out for Princess Leia, Yoda, and even Darth Vader.

It feels real

The ride takes place on a flight simulator, the same type used to train astronauts and pilots. The combination of the simulator and movie makes it feel like you are really rocketing through space.

Hang on tight

Just like the old version, the Star Tours adventure has sharp turns and lots of bumpy thrills. Don't eat anything just before you ride.

You must be at least 40 inches tall to experience Star Tours.

The Reader Review

A Great Big Beautiful Day!

By: Devon, age 9
Robbinsville, NJ

This is a must-ride for all. C-3P0 is your pilot as you zoom toward different planets. And it's all in 3-D. You cannot miss this ride!

Walt Disney: One Man's Dream

You probably know a lot about Mickey Mouse — he has a pup named Pluto, he loves red shorts, and Minnie is his favorite gal. But how much do you know about the man who created him? You can learn a lot about Walt Disney at this attraction. He's the man who started The Walt Disney Company.

Take your time

Lots of Walt's belongings are on display in the pre-show area. Look for special items like old family photos, his piano, and the Academy Award he won for *Snow White and the Seven Dwarfs*. Spend some time exploring the exhibits before you see the movie.

Fun fact

Did you know that Mickey Mouse wasn't Walt's first famous cartoon character? A rabbit named Oswald was. But Walt's plans for Oswald didn't quite work out. Luckily, he never gave up, or he never would have created Mickey!

To learn more about Walt Disney, turn back to page 8 of this book.

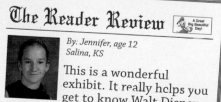

The Reader Review

A Great Big Beautiful Day!

By: Jennifer, age 12
Salina, KS

This is a wonderful exhibit. It really helps you get to know Walt Disney and the magic that he brought to the world.

HOT TiP!

If you want to meet the characters from Disney•Pixar films, head straight to Pixar Place!

Pizza Planet Arcade

This arcade and pizza restaurant is like Andy's favorite hangout from *Toy Story*. It is near the Muppet*Vision 3-D attraction, by the Miss Piggy fountain.

There are lots of games to try here. You can even challenge "The Claw." If you beat it, you win a small prize. It costs extra to play here — your parents need to buy tokens before you can start.

When your tummy starts rumbling, you can grab a bite to eat. Pizza Planet sells pizza, cookies, lemonade, and other munchies.

The American Idol® Experience

In the TV version of *American Idol*, contestants sing their hearts out for the judges. At The American Idol Experience, they sing for you! Yep, the audience members are the judges here. In each show, three park guests (age 14 and older) try to dazzle the audience with their musical talent. Some guests have more talent than others — but most of them are very good. The show takes place several times a day.

HOT TIP!

The Indiana Jones Epic Stunt Spectacular is a noisy show! If explosions and other loud noises hurt your ears, sit in the back of the theater. It's not as loud there.

Reader Tip

"Outside of Indiana Jones, there is a sign that says 'Do not pull the rope.' Ignore the sign and pull the rope! You'll be glad you did."

Cameron (age 10)
Naples, FL

LOUD
Attraction Reaction

Disney's Hollywood Studios

DISNEY'S
FASTPASS

Indiana Jones Epic Stunt Spectacular

Fire, explosions, daring escapes, and other special effects are the stars of this attraction. Stunt men and stunt women act out scenes from the movie *Raiders of the Lost Ark* and show how special effects are done. The audience watches from a large theater, and adults are chosen to perform with the pros. (It is too dangerous for kids.)

Fun for everyone

All the surprises keep everyone on the edge of their seats. One of the best parts of the show is the re-creation of the scene in the movie where the giant ball rolls down and seems to crush Indiana Jones. Even though you know it's a stunt, it seems quite real.

Don't try this at home

Stunt people act out the scenes and then explain how each of the stunts was performed. They make it look easy, but it is not.

The Reader Review

A Great Big Beautiful Day!

By: Philip, age 11
Palm Harbor, FL

This is great for anyone who likes stunts, action, adventure, and Indiana Jones movies. It's my favorite show at Walt Disney World.

HOT TiP!

Toy Story Mania always has a long line. Try to snag a Fastpass or get there first thing in the morning.

Toy Story Mania!

#10 RIDE READER PLEASER

If you think Buzz Lightyear's Space Ranger Spin is a blast, you will love Toy Story Mania! It's like jumping into a life-size video game. It also makes you feel like you're the size of a toy as you travel through some super colorful rooms — all while aiming your special shooter at cool targets.

Of course, this high-tech ride has a twist: All guests wear 3-D glasses. That makes all of the special effects really pop. As you rack up points and trigger surprises, you'll be cheered on by Woody, Buzz, Jessie, Rex, Hamm, and lots of other *Toy Story* stars.

Toy Story Mania is good for gamers of all ages and skill levels. So if you are a beginner, don't worry. You'll get better every time you play. In fact, we're pretty sure you'll be giving pointers to your parents.

The Reader Review

A Great Big Beautiful Day!

By: Rory, age 11
Rochester, NY

I love this ride! The 3-D effects make you think you are really in the game. Be sure to get a Fastpass before they are all gone!

PHOTO BY JILL SAFRO

Entertainment

Lights! Camera! Action! There's a lot of star-studded entertainment at Disney's Hollywood Studios. Most of it has a TV or movie theme. Two of the best shows are described below.

FASTPASS

CITIZENS OF HOLLYWOOD

If you take a walk on this park's Hollywood or Sunset boulevard, you might run into performers called Citizens of Hollywood. They play the parts of movie stars, policemen, cab drivers, reporters, and other funny characters from the 1930s and 1940s. They love to talk to theme park guests, so don't be shy. You will feel like you are a part of the show!

LOUD
Attraction Reaction

DARK
Attraction Reaction

SCARY
Attraction Reaction

FANTASMIC!

What does Mickey Mouse dream about? You can find out at Fantasmic! It's an amazing show that combines water, laser lights, Disney characters, movies, music, and a little magic.

Mickey's dreams are fun to watch — but some of them are a little scary. (Disney villains keep turning his dreams into nightmares.) In the end, good wins over evil and Mickey's dreams are happy once more.

Fantasmic is presented in a theater beside a lake near the Tower of Terror. It's very popular, so be sure to line up at least an hour before the show starts. And, if it isn't summer, bring a jacket or a sweater — it can get chilly! If you sit near the front, you might get a little bit wet. The lake gets lit on fire, too. Check a park Times Guide to see what nights Fantasmic! is performed.

UMBRELLA FUN

There is a very special umbrella in this park. It is attached to a lamp post near the Lights, Motors, Action attraction. What's so special about it? If you grab the handle and stand on the black square, you will be showered with a surprise. Feel free to sing in the rain!

Where to find
Characters
at DISNEY'S HOLLYWOOD STUDIOS

There are lots of places to meet Disney and Pixar characters at Disney's Hollywood Studios. One of the best spots is the **Streets of America**. Characters such as Phineas, Ferb, Mater, and Lightning McQueen meet with guests throughout the day. You can get a ton of pictures.

Where's Mickey? That's a good question! He pops up in places all over the park. Ask a cast member or check a guidemap to find out where he'll be during your visit, so you can stop by and say hello.

Buzz, Woody, and Jessie from *Toy Story* have their very own spot for meeting guests. You can pose for pictures with them and characters from other Disney•Pixar flicks on **Pixar Place**. Ask them to sign the autograph section at the end of this book.

Disney's Hollywood Studios

Arrive at Disney's Hollywood Studios before the opening time. The gates often open a few minutes ahead of the scheduled time.

Bring this book to the park. When you run into characters, you'll have something for them to sign!

There are "chicken exits" at both Tower of Terror and Rock 'n' Roller Coaster, just in case you change your mind at the last minute.

Don't eat a thing for at least an hour before you ride Rock 'n' Roller Coaster, Star Tours, or the Twilight Zone Tower of Terror.

Some stage shows don't open until late morning. Be sure to check a Times Guide for exact show times.

Some folks think the number 13 is scary. But if the wait time at Tower of Tower is listed as 13 minutes, there is probably a much shorter wait — and that's not scary at all!

The Streets of America area is a good place to meet characters.

The front rows at Fantasmic! get a little wet. The best seats are in the back at either end of the theater.

See Toy Story Mania and Star Tours — The Adventures Continue in the morning, before the lines get long. Get a Fastpass assignment if you can.

Attraction Ratings

REALLY COOL
(Don't Miss)

- Indiana Jones Epic Stunt Spectacular
- Studio Backlot Tour
- Fantasmic!
- Lights, Motors, Action! Extreme Stunt Show
- The American Idol Experience
- The Magic of Disney Animation

THE COOLEST
(See at Least Twice)

- Toy Story Mania!
- Muppet*Vision 3-D
- Star Tours — The Adventures Continue
- The Twilight Zone Tower of Terror
- Beauty and the Beast — Live on Stage
- Rock 'n' Roller Coaster
- Voyage of The Little Mermaid

COOL
(Check It Out)

- The Great Movie Ride
- Honey, I Shrunk the Kids Movie Set Adventure
- Disney Junior — Live on Stage!
- Walt Disney: One Man's Dream

Your favorite Disney's Hollywood Studios attractions

Disney's Animal Kingdom

PHOTO BY MIKE CARROLL

Animal Kingdom celebrates animals of every kind, from lions, tigers, and zebras to giant turtles whose ancestors lived during the time of the dinosaurs. And they're all real! You may get closer to them than you've ever been before. There are dinosaurs, too. The dinos aren't real, but they sure seem to be.

Animal Kingdom is a theme park with many attractions. Just like the Magic Kingdom, there are different "lands" to visit in Animal Kingdom. The major lands are called Discovery Island, Asia, Africa, and DinoLand U.S.A.

You enter the park through The Oasis. It's a big garden with plants and animals. Take some time to look around. Then cross a bridge to Discovery Island, admire the giant Tree of Life, and decide which land to explore first.

What's the best way to see Animal Kingdom? Use this map to help you decide!

AFRICA

A Kilimanjaro Safaris

B Pangani Forest
   Exploration Trail

C Wildlife Express to
   Rafiki's Planet Watch

D Rafiki's Planet Watch

E Festival of the Lion King

DISCOVERY ISLAND

F The Tree of Life

G Discovery Island Trails

H It's Tough to be a Bug!

ASIA

I Flights of Wonder at Caravan Stage

J Maharajah Jungle Trek

K Kali River Rapids

L Expedition Everest

DINOLAND U.S.A.

M Dinosaur

N The Boneyard playground

O Finding Nemo — The Musical

P Chester & Hester's Dino–Rama!

Discovery Island

Discovery Island is the gateway to all the other lands in the park. (It used to be called Safari Village.) The Tree of Life stands near the center of Discovery Island. If you wander around its roots, you'll see all kinds of animals.

Hidden Mickey Alert!

There's a mouse in the moss! Look for clusters of moss near the tiger on The Tree of Life. They form a Hidden Mickey.

PHOTO BY MIKE CARROLL

The Tree of Life

This man-made tree is 145 feet tall. From far away it looks like any other tree. But when you get up close, you'll realize that this is not an ordinary tree. It's covered with animals!

Artists have carved 325 animal images into its trunk. In fact, it's called The Tree of Life because it's covered with so many different kinds of animal life. The lion is easy to see. Other animals, such as the ant and dolphin, are a lot harder to spot. How many can you find?

The Reader Review

A Great Big Beautiful Day!

By: John, age 14
Washington Township, NJ

Once inside Animal Kingdom, you can't miss The Tree of Life. Trying to spot all the animals on the tree is nearly impossible! A great place to search for animals is while in line for It's Tough to be a Bug!

Reader Tip

"At It's Tough to be a Bug, be sure to sit back straight in your chair so you won't miss a thing."

**Chelsea (age 12)
Howell, NJ**

HOT TiP!

If you hate creepy crawlers, skip It's Tough to be a Bug!

It's Tough to be a Bug!

PHOTO BY JILL SAFRO

The Tree of Life has a hollow trunk. It's cool, dark, and roomy inside. That makes it a great place to watch a 3-D movie called It's Tough to be a Bug! It's hosted by Flik, the star of *A Bug's Life*. Most of these bugs are friendly and funny. But when Flik's enemy Hopper makes an appearance, the show gets a little bit scary.

This movie is about the tiny creatures that outnumber all others on our planet — bugs. In it, animated insects use music and special effects to show how hard their lives are. They also try to show humans just how important bugs really are. This show is much too scary for some younger kids.

The Reader Review

A Great Big Beautiful Day!

By: Benjamin, age 11
East Providence, RI

I am not a big fan of insects, so I found this show very suspenseful. You never know where the bugs are going to pop up next! The effects are great, right down to the Audio-Animatronics Flik and Hopper.

Disney's Animal Kingdom

DinoLand U.S.A.

The entrance to this land is marked by a big dinosaur skeleton. Inside, you will find life-like dinosaurs as well as live animals that have existed since prehistoric times. The main attraction is Dinosaur, but there are lots of other things to see and do. For a hand-clapping good time, catch Finding Nemo — The Musical. In DinoLand you can also dig for bones in an amazing playground, learn about real dinosaurs, or take a spin on a friendly dino ride.

Chester & Hester's Dino-Rama!

Dino-Rama is inside DinoLand U.S.A. It's a dino-themed fair, complete with carnival games and two rides. (It costs money to play the games, but you can enjoy the rides as much as you want without paying an extra penny.)

TriceraTop Spin

The dinos that soar on this ride look like they're part of an antique wind-up toy. Just like at Dumbo the Flying Elephant and the Magic Carpets of Aladdin, riders here can control how high or low their TriceraTops go. Younger kids love this attraction.

Primeval Whirl

Speedy little cars race around the track on this mini roller coaster. Each car spins and bumps as it moves, which makes for a wild trip. You must be at least 48 inches tall to ride.

PHOTO BY JILL SAFRO

Dinosaur

This thrilling and scary ride takes guests back to the last few minutes of the Earth's Cretaceous Period. (That is when the dinosaurs died out.)

Save the dinosaur

The mission on Dinosaur is to save the last iguanodon. You have to brave a meteor shower and the largest Audio-Animatronics creature Disney has ever made. It's a dinosaur called

a carnotaurus, and it may be the ugliest thing you've ever seen. This monster has the face of a toad, horns like a bull, and squirrel-like arms. It looks like it's alive. The nostrils even move as it breathes. And, boy, can it run. The carnotaurus runs for about 30 feet. Be careful! This hungry monster is not just after the iguanodon — it wants to eat *you*, too.

An exciting (and scary) ride

Most kids agree that this is a very exciting ride, but one that might not be for everyone. Kids who don't like scary rides can find some tamer dinos on TriceraTop Spin. But for kids who like to be scared, Dinosaur is a must.

You must be at least 40 inches tall to ride Dinosaur.

The Reader Review

By: Samantha, age 13
Churubusco, IN

I love Dinosaur! The dinosaurs, darkness, and roughness make the ride extra exciting. It only lasts a few minutes, but it seemed a lot longer to me. If you like rough rides, this is one of the roughest!

Reader Tip

"Dinosaur is very loud and dark, and it really jerks and pulls you around. Some young kids won't like it at all!"

Julia (age 11)
Prairieville, LA

Finding Nemo — The Musical

Uh-oh. Nemo has wandered off *again*. Will he never learn?! We hope not, since this show tells his story in a whole new way — with music. There are lots of peppy tunes to sing along with during the performance. High-flying acrobats, colorful puppets, and talented dancers round out the show.

The action takes place in DinoLand's Theater in the Wild. The show happens inside a building, but it seems like it's under water. You won't get wet, though, since it's all done with special effects.

The 40-minute musical show is presented several times a day. Check a park Times Guide for the schedule. It's a popular show — arrive early. The theater is air-conditioned, so you can cool off while Nemo and his friends entertain. The show is a bit long for young kids.

The Reader Review

A Great Big Beautiful Day!

By: Riley, age 12
Dayton, OH

I don't love shows that much — but the giant fish are pretty neat! Overall, I think Finding Nemo — The Musical is best for Nemo fans.

The Boneyard

Are you ready to jump into the biggest sandbox you've ever seen? It's here, and it's filled with bones! You can uncover the bones of a mammoth and find clues about how the animal died.

There are also dinosaur footprints that roar when you jump in them and a xylophone that's made of dinosaur bones. There's a rope maze for climbing and plenty of slippery slides, too. Be sure to check out the Olden-gate Bridge. It looks like a dinosaur skeleton.

The Reader Review

A Great Big Beautiful Day!

By: Olivia, age 9
Watertown, WI

My brother is 5 years old and he had a better time at The Boneyard than I did. There's lots to do, but I couldn't wait to ride Dinosaur!

HOT TiP!

The xylophone is next to the trunk in The Boneyard playground. Press the bones to make a sound.

Africa

Before creating this land, Disney Imagineers spent months on the continent of Africa learning all about the plants and animals there. When they came back, they made an African forest and a grassland in Florida. Then they filled it with hundreds of the same animals they had seen in Africa. Most of the animals in Animal Kingdom came from special parks and zoos around the world. You can see many animals on a safari ride and learn all about them at Rafiki's Planet Watch.

Kilimanjaro Safaris

In this wild jungle adventure, you ride in a vehicle that is wide open. There's almost nothing between you and the animals. You may see hippos, lions, giraffes, rhinos, elephants, and more. Some animals may even come up close. But don't worry — dangerous animals can't get near you. It is perfectly safe.

This attraction got a new addition a few years back — zebras! Keep your eyes peeled for these beautiful creatures. And have your camera ready at all times. You can take a lot of great photos in these parts.

The Reader Review
A Great Big Beautiful Day!

By: William, age 10
Glen Ellyn, IL

Kilimanjaro Safaris took my family and me to Africa! I really like that some animals can come up to your truck. I recommend this attraction to kids of all ages and anyone who likes animals.

PHOTO BY JILL SAFRO

Pangani Forest Exploration Trail

After you take a ride on the Kilimanjaro Safaris, go for a walk on the Pangani Forest Exploration Trail. This nature trail is filled with many exciting sights. You'll come nose-to-nose with a naked mole rat and look for hippos underwater. Exotic fish and birds live in the African Aviary.

No binoculars necessary

Pick up a bird guide (they should be hanging on a post in the aviary) and see how many different birds you can spot. Afterward, make a stop at the meerkat exhibit. Some people call it the "Timon exhibit" because he's a meerkat. (There are no Pumbaas here, though. Meerkats and warthogs don't get along in real life.)

Greetings, gorillas

At the end of the trail, you see a family of gorillas. They are usually hanging out on the hills or playing. You might even spot a baby gorilla in the group.

HOT TiP!

After you pet the animals at Affection Section, don't forget to wash your hands. Use the special sink that's near the exit.

Rafiki's Planet Watch

A train called the Wildlife Express is the only way to get to Rafiki's Planet Watch. (Hop aboard in Africa.) During the ride, you get a behind-the-scenes look at the buildings where animals from the safari ride are cared for.

Lend a helping hand

The exhibits at Rafiki's Planet Watch teach you what animals need to survive — and what people can do to help. There is an animal hospital, places for animals to get special care, and lots of shows meant to get you excited about conservation. There are even ways to find out about some conservation projects near your home. It's also a great place to meet Rafiki and get an autograph.

Talk to the animals

Many exhibits at Rafiki's Planet Watch are interactive. In Song of the Rain Forest, you are surrounded by sounds you might hear in a real rain forest. At the Hallway of Animal Health and Care, you can sometimes watch doctors care for animals. People can walk among animals like goats and sheep in the Affection Section. It is okay to pet them, but feeding is not allowed.

Festival of the Lion King

This is one spectacular musical show. Even if you have the movie memorized, you are in for a few surprises. Many of the characters from the film are here, but they look a bit different. Most of them are played by humans dressed in colorful African costumes.

An action-packed performance

The theater has big stages that look like parade floats. (That's because they were once used in a parade at Disneyland.) On one, Simba sits atop Pride Rock. The wisecracking Pumbaa sits on another. Gymnasts dressed like monkeys jump and do tricks.

The mighty jungle

After singers and dancers perform some of the best songs from *The Lion King*, it's time for the big finale. Stilt walkers, acrobats, and dancers join in for an exciting version of "The Lion Sleeps Tonight." Even the audience gets in on the act, so get ready to clap and sing!

This show moved to the Africa section of Animal Kingdom in 2014.

The Reader Review

By: Erin, age 10
Weippe, ID

The Festival of the Lion King is toe-tapping, sing-along fun for all ages. And there's acrobatics aplenty. Enjoy the show!

Who am I?

- I am 10 years old.
- I have a big sister and a baby brother.
- I can run super fast.

Answer: Dash Parr

Asia

Asia is the largest continent on Earth. It's almost twice as big as North America! The land called Asia in Animal Kingdom is a lot smaller than the real thing, but gives you an idea of what the Asian continent is like. It has jungles and rain forests and magnificent animals. It's also home to the fastest raging river in Animal Kingdom. If you want to get wet, you can shoot the rapids down the river on a ride called Kali River Rapids. And for one of the most exciting experiences of all, ride Expedition Everest! For a calmer experience, check out the Flights of Wonder show.

Maharajah Jungle Trek

Put on your walking shoes and keep your eyes peeled. This jungle trail is the place to spot scaly animals called Komodo dragons, plus deer, giant fruit bats (they eat melon), and tigers. You'll also see colorful birds along the way and tons of plants and trees. Pick up a map at the beginning of the trail to know what to look for.

You see the bats about halfway through your walk. Their wings are enormous! In some places, there is no glass between you and the bats. But don't worry — they're not interested in humans. Still, it might be creepy to stand so close to them. If the bats make you uncomfortable, there's a window outside the building that lets you observe them from a distance.

PHOTO BY JILL SAFRO

Hidden Mickey Alert!
The mural by the tigers is where this Mickey head is hiding.

The Reader Review

By: Sam, age 9
Eatontown, NJ

This is a very intense roller coaster. When you go backwards, keep your head back so you don't bounce around too much. The beginning is pretty relaxing, but you are in for some big surprises!

A Great Big Beautiful Day!

Reader Tip

"Remember to bring a water bottle with you to Animal Kingdom on hot days."

Meg (age 12)
Vero Beach, FL

READER
#2 RIDE
PLEASER

DARK
Attraction Reaction

SCARY
Attraction Reaction

WILD
Attraction Reaction

Expedition Everest

Disney's FASTPASS

Mount Everest is the tallest mountain in the world. Can you guess the name of the tallest mountain in Walt Disney World? If you said Expedition Everest, you are right! Of course, it is much more than a mountain. It's a thrilling train ride through forests and waterfalls and over snowcapped mountain peaks. This train ride is a lot rougher than Big Thunder Mountain.

Here, you not only travel forward and backward through caverns and canyons, you also whiz by an angry yeti (that's an abominable snowman). His job is to protect the mountain from you!

This attraction is not for everyone. If you love wild, crazy, dark, and *scary* rides — and are at least 44 inches tall — give it a try. And be sure to say hello to the yeti for us!

The Reader Review

By: Cameron, age 9
Naples, FL

I enjoy this fast-moving water ride. I really like the waterfall, but not the fire. It can scare some kids. It's fun when people shoot water at you, too.

Reader Tip

"Everything you carry on Kali River Rapids will get soaked. And so will you!"

Drew (age 12)
Jenison, MI

Kali River Rapids

This is one of the wettest and wildest rides in Walt Disney World. Don't bother trying to pick a dry seat on the raft, because everyone gets wet! It begins as a peaceful raft trip through a rain forest. But things don't stay calm for very long. The raft bumps along down the river, spinning and turning every time it hits a rock.

Along the way you catch a glimpse of how logging (cutting down trees for lumber) can destroy the rain forest. Don't be scared if you see a fire — that's just part of the ride. You avoid the burning logs, but will you be safe from the waterfall? We won't tell. (You might want to bring a towel, just in case.)

Guests must be at least 38 inches tall to ride the rapids.

PHOTO BY JILL SAFRO

Disney's Animal Kingdom

HOT TIP!

Want to keep your stuff dry while you ride Kali River Rapids? Leave it in a locker near the ride's entrance. The lockers are free for up to 2 hours.

Who am I?

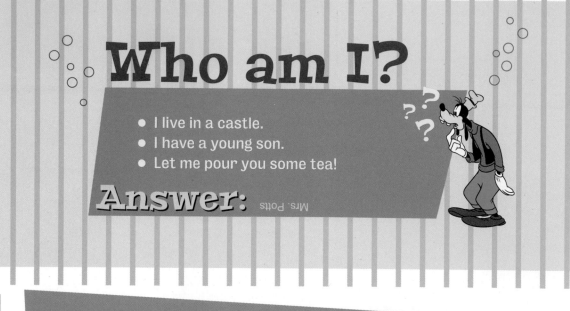

- I live in a castle.
- I have a young son.
- Let me pour you some tea!

Answer: Mrs. Potts

Flights of Wonder

Live birds are the stars of this high-flying show that takes place on the Caravan Stage. They swoop and soar and do amazing tricks. Sometimes one of the performers is an African gray parrot named Quasar. He's a whiz at math!

This show is presented several times each day. It lasts about 25 minutes. Check a park Times Guide for the schedule. And don't leave right away — sometimes a handler will bring a bird out to meet guests after the show. Flights of Wonder is fun for guests of all ages.

The theater is covered, but there is no air-conditioning.

Wilderness Explorers

In the movie *Up*, Russell is a dedicated Wilderness Explorer. He wants to earn as many merit badges as he can. Now you can become a Wilderness Explorer, too. Start by heading to Wilderness Explorer Headquarters at the Oasis bridge. After you take the official pledge, you will get field guides describing different challenges. Complete a challenge and earn a badge! There are about 30 different badges in all. There is no extra charge to become an Animal Kingdom Wilderness Explorer, and the badges are free. It's fun for the whole family.

Entertainment

Don't be surprised if the performers at Animal Kingdom come right up to you. Some walk on two legs, while others walk on four — or eight. There's a parade, plus drummers, live animals, and many other things to entertain you along the way. Read all about some of them below.

AFRICAN ENTERTAINMENT

Drummers perform in Harambe throughout the day. There's a covered area where you can listen to them and escape the blazing sun.

Gi-Tar Dan

A talented world traveler named Gi-Tar Dan entertains guests at Rafiki's Planet Watch. Each of Dan's 20-minute shows involves singing, guitar-playing, and storytelling. He may even sing a special song just for you. Check a park Times Guide for Gi-Tar Dan's show schedule.

HOT TiP!

Animal Kingdom can get very hot — even hotter than the other theme parks. Be sure to drink lots of water.

DIVINE

You may think your eyes are playing tricks on you when you see this giant plant start to walk through the park! The plant is actually a very talented performer walking on stilts.

113

Where to find Characters at DISNEY'S ANIMAL KINGDOM

It's easy to find Disney characters at Animal Kingdom — they have special spots to greet guests all over the park. **Adventurers Outpost** on Discovery Island is the best place to meet Mickey and Minnie. They are there all day. Ask them to sign the autograph section at the end of this book.

Rafiki, Chip, and Dale mingle with folks at **Rafiki's Planet Watch**. Look for Goofy and Pluto at **Chester & Hester's Dino-Rama** in DinoLand U.S.A. Donald hangs out near the **Cretaceous Trail**. Russell and Dug greet guests by the entrance to **It's Tough to be a Bug!** And you could run into Pooh, Baloo, and King Louie while exploring **Discovery Island**. Locations sometimes change, so be on the lookout!

114

Animal Kingdom

Animal Kingdom can get very hot, especially in the summer months. Head for Festival of the Lion King, Finding Nemo — The Musical, Kali River Rapids, or Rafiki's Planet Watch to cool off. And don't forget to drink lots of water.

Go to the thrill rides — Expedition Everest, Dinosaur, and Kali River Rapids — early, before they get too crowded, and try to get a Fastpass.

On the Kilimanjaro Safaris ride, look at the chart over your head. The pictures will show you which animals you're about to see.

Check the Tip Board on Discovery Island to find out how long the wait is for the most popular attractions.

It doesn't really matter what time you get to the safari — the animals are there all day long.

It's Tough to be a Bug is very scary to some kids (especially younger ones and those who don't like the dark). In it, bugs seem to shoot quills and stinky smells, giant spiders dangle from the ceiling, and creepy critters seem to scamper beneath the seats. If you get creeped out during the show, just grab your parent and leave early.

It's fun to see how many animals you can find carved into The Tree of Life and the other buildings on Discovery Island.

Look for Mickey and Minnie at the Adventurers Outpost on Discovery Island. Bring your camera!

Can't find your parents? Ask the closest Disney cast member for help.

Stash your stuff in a locker before riding Kali River Rapids — unless you don't mind if it gets wet!

Attraction Ratings

THE COOLEST
(See at Least Twice)

- Expedition Everest
- Kilimanjaro Safaris
- Kali River Rapids
- Festival of the Lion King
- Dinosaur
- Pangani Forest Exploration Trail
- Maharajah Jungle Trek

REALLY COOL
(Don't Miss)

- The Boneyard playground
- It's Tough to be a Bug!
- Flights of Wonder
- Song of the Rain Forest (at Rafiki's Planet Watch)
- Primeval Whirl

COOL
(Check It Out)

- The Oasis
- Affection Section (at Rafiki's Planet Watch)
- TriceraTop Spin
- Finding Nemo — The Musical

Your favorite Animal Kingdom attractions

Everything Else in the World

No matter what you're interested in — water fun, sports, or animals — Walt Disney World has enough to make every minute of your vacation a blast. After you visit the theme parks, there's still so much to do. There are water parks, speedy boats to rent, horses to ride, a gigantic arcade, and lots of neat shopping spots.

If you are into sports, be sure to check out the ESPN Wide World of Sports complex, rent a bike, or try your hand at miniature golf. To test your detective skills, join one of Disney World's special scavenger hunts.

In this chapter, you can read up on all the extra activities and find out about hotels and restaurants at Walt Disney World. Then you can help your family decide where to stay, where to eat, and what to do when you're not at the theme parks.

Waters of the World

It's easy to get wet, stay cool, and have fun at Walt Disney World. That's because it's a water wonderland. Choose a water park or take a dip in your hotel pool. If you're under the age of 10, you must have a grown-up with you to enter the water parks.

Typhoon Lagoon

A typhoon is a powerful, windy storm. It dumps huge amounts of rain and sends objects flying through the air. This water park looks like a typhoon hit it. There's even a boat stuck on a mountaintop! Of course, a storm didn't really put the boat there — Disney Imagineers did. They also put in pools, waterslides, and a raft ride.

Catch the wave

The big pool here is like a small ocean. It has 6-foot waves! That makes body-surfing tons of fun. There are speed slides to try, too. In the mood for a thrill? Try Crush 'n' Gusher. It's like a water roller coaster. For a calmer experience, you can hop into a tube and float along a lazy river. There's also a special area just for younger kids — Ketchakiddee Creek. It has small slides and other games.

Swim with sharks

Shark Reef is an amazing part of Typhoon Lagoon. It's the home of bonnethead and leopard sharks. And you can swim with them. Don't worry — they are friendly sharks. They don't mind when people swim in their tank. Are you brave enough to swim with the sharks? (There's no age restriction, but you will have to wear a life jacket.)

HOT TiP

Bring water shoes to WDW parks. That way, you can play in the interactive fountains without ruining your shoes.

Blizzard Beach

Would you wear a bathing suit to a snow-covered mountain? Probably not. But you should wear one to Blizzard Beach. It looks like a place to ski, but it's really a water park. So don't worry if you can't ski. Nobody skis down the mountain here. They slide!

Reach the peak

Like a real ski resort, all the action centers around a mountain. In this case, it's Mount Gushmore. To get to the top, you can take a chairlift. The ride gives you a great view of the park. The scariest slide on the mountain is Summit Plummet. It begins 120 feet in the air, on a platform that looks like a ski jump. It drops you down a steep slide at about 60 miles per hour. That's faster than many cars go on the highway.

Slip-sliding away

There are plenty of other ways to slide down the mountain. Tube slides, body slides, and inner-tube rides can keep you busy all day long. It's fun to splash in the wave pool, too. For preteens, there's Ski Patrol Training Camp, with its "iceberg" obstacle course and ropes for swinging into the water. Tike's Peak is a special place for younger kids. It has slides and a snow-castle fountain play area.

Reader Tip

"Go to a water park early in the day — when it's hot and crowded at the theme parks. Then you can return to the theme park when it cools down in the evening."

David (age 14)
Calabasas, CA

Fort Wilderness

Fort Wilderness is tucked away in a wooded area of Walt Disney World. (It isn't really a fort. It's a campground.) You can stay overnight or just come for a day. There are tennis and volleyball courts, and a marina with lots of boats. You could spend days here and not run out of things to do. If you don't have too much time, you could stop in at the pony farm or rent a boat for a ride around Bay Lake.

Pony Farm

There is a small farm at Fort Wilderness. It's a short walk from Pioneer Hall. There is no charge to visit the farm, but there is a small fee to go for a pony ride. Be sure to bring a grown-up with you. If you don't want to ride a pony, you can still stop by and say hello. Most kids think a visit to the farm is a fun way to spend some time away from the theme parks — especially if they are animal lovers.

More Fort Wilderness Fun

Fort Wilderness offers lots of other things to do. You can rent a canoe for a trip along some canals. Or you can rent a bicycle and explore one of the many trails. At the Tri-Circle-D Ranch, you can see the horses that pull the trolleys in the Magic Kingdom. (They live in a barn near Pioneer Hall.)

Kids over 9 years old can take a trail ride on horseback. You can also enjoy a wagon ride, go fishing, or roast marshmallows at a campfire with Chip and Dale.

Sports

Kids who like sports can find plenty of ways to keep active at Walt Disney World. You can rent boats and bikes at one of the resorts, or play miniature golf on one of Disney's themed courses. To see athletes at work, visit the ESPN Wide World of Sports complex. Read on to find out how.

Speed Boats

A Sea Raycer is a speedy little motorboat that you can rent. And it delivers big thrills. If you are at least 12 years old and five feet tall, you can drive one yourself. How cool is that?

These zippy boat rides get very high marks from kids. The boat goes surprisingly fast and the ride can be bumpy, especially if you drive over a wave caused by another boat. So hang on tight. And drive carefully — there is a lot of boat traffic out there.

You can rent a Sea Raycer at many Disney resorts. The cost is about $35 for a half hour.

Everything Else in the World

ESPN Wide World of Sports Complex

Major sports nuts might enjoy a visit to this complex. It has facilities for every sport you can imagine. The Atlanta Braves baseball team comes here for spring training (in March).

You can spend a day watching some amateur events. Tickets to the complex cost about $12 for kids ages 3 through 9 and about $17 for anyone 10 or older. If you want to see a professional game, you have to buy your tickets ahead of time. The prices vary. Have a parent call 407-939-4263 for information.

HOT TiP!
The baseball stadium has lawn seating. Bring a blanket and have a picnic while you watch the game.

Miniature Golf

Even if you've never held a golf club before, you'll do well at mini-golf. It's fun to play and full of surprises.

Fantasia Gardens

If you have seen the old movie *Fantasia*, you'll know how this miniature golf course got its name. Where else will you find hippos on tiptoe, dancing mushrooms, or xylophone stairs?

The holes are grouped by musical themes. At the Dance of the Hours hole, watch the hippo standing on an alligator. If you hit the ball through the gator's mouth, the hippo dances!

The cost is about $11 to play one round for kids ages 3 through 9 and about $13 for anyone 10 or older.

Disney's Winter Summerland

Sometimes even Santa Claus needs a vacation. Just like you, he picked Walt Disney World as the perfect place to go and have fun.

As the story goes, Santa and his helpers built these mini-golf courses as a place to relax and enjoy the sun. That's why one looks like a beach, with sand castles and surfboards on it. But then the elves got homesick, so they built a second course that reminded them of the North Pole. Everything looks like it is covered in snow. There are even igloos, jolly snowmen, and holes for ice fishing.

For a bit of a challenge, try the summer course. It's a little harder than the winter course. Santa is snoozing at one of the trickiest holes. You have to hit the ball across his lap without waking him up. The winter holes offer fun surprises, too. Get the ball in one of the holes and Mickey himself pops out of a present!

It costs about $11 to play on one course for kids ages 3 to 9 and about $13 for anyone 10 or older.

Scavenger Hunts

If you are a fan of the tales told by Walt Disney World's shows and rides, you'll probably enjoy these special tours. Each one makes you feel like you are part of the story.

Family Magic Tour

This program is fun for the whole family. Parents and kids can join in a themed scavenger hunt through the Magic Kingdom. Guests search for the answers to different clues that lead to the missing item.

If you go on this two-hour tour, be sure to wear your sneakers — you will be doing lots of walking! The cost is about $34 for everyone age 3 and over. Parents should call 407-WDW-TOUR (939-8687) to make reservations.

Pirate Adventure

Did you know that there is pirates' treasure buried at Walt Disney World? Some is hidden in the Seven Seas Lagoon. (That's near the Magic Kingdom.) A few times a week, an expedition just for kids sails out from the Grand Floridian in search of it.

There are pirate adventures at the Caribbean Beach resort, Yacht and Beach Club, and at the Port Orleans resorts, too.

Do you think you are up to the challenge of a treasure hunt? The captain of the ship will give you a map and a series of puzzling clues to help you on your way. During the journey, kids get to eat a light snack.

You have two hours to find the treasure. And if you do, it's yours to keep! These programs are for kids ages 4 to 12. Cost is about $34 per child. Parents should call 407-939-3463 for reservations.

Downtown Disney

What has shops and restaurants, movies, games, and much more? Downtown Disney! (Its name may change to Disney Springs in 2015.) Just like before, there are lots of cool areas for kids to explore.

HOT TiP!

DisneyQuest is a great place to head to when it's rainy outside. You can spend hours in there.

The West Side

This zone has places to shop, eat, go bowling (at a place called Splitsville), and catch a movie, plus DisneyQuest (read all about it on the next page).

There's even a show by Cirque du Soleil (pronounced: *serk due so-LAY*). It's performed in a building that looks like a giant circus tent — but this show's not like an ordinary circus. There are lots of gymnasts and acrobats dressed in colorful costumes. They twist their bodies and dance in unusual ways. Parents can buy tickets by calling 407-939-7600 or visiting *disneyworld.com/cirque*.

Marketplace

Searching for a souvenir? Be sure to visit the Marketplace. There are lots of shops there. One spot that kids love is World of Disney. It's jam-packed with Disney-themed goodies. The Once Upon a Toy store has a design your own Mr. Potato Head station. You can also make a wacky creation at the Lego store. (It's okay just to play — you don't have to buy.)

More to explore

Downtown Disney is growing every day. Be sure to look for new surprises during your visit.

Hidden Mickey Alert!

Some of the Marketplace's dancing water fountains form the shape of you-know-who!

DisneyQuest

This place is probably bigger than any arcade you've ever seen. In fact, some folks call it an "indoor interactive theme park." It's filled from top to bottom with every game imaginable. To get in, you'll need a ticket. Ask your parents to call to check prices (407-W-DISNEY).

Pick a floor, any floor

DisneyQuest has five floors full of games. Once you are inside (and have paid your admission fee), you won't have to pay to play most games. Here are some of the cooler areas for you to explore:

Pirates of the Caribbean — Battle for Buccaneer Gold: A virtual pirate voyage, this game lets you steer a ship, fire cannons, and race for gold.

Virtual Jungle Cruise: Hop on a raft with other team members, plunge down a prehistoric river (watch out for dinosaurs!), and try to avoid being splashed.

CyberSpace Mountain: Are you a fan of the Magic Kingdom's Space Mountain? If so, head for CyberSpace Mountain! It is a "virtual" version of the Tomorrowland coaster. And you get to design the ride! It can be as scary or as tame as you want. (Do not do this right after you eat.)

Buzz Lightyear's Astroblaster: Here you can pilot a futuristic bumper car and fire balls at other drivers — while you try to avoid getting blasted yourself.

Animation Academy: This spot shows you what it is like to be an animator. An expert will offer tips on how to draw a Disney character.

Take a break

Kids agree that you could spend a few hours playing here. Try out all the games and activities — but don't hog them. Be sure to give others a chance to enjoy favorites, too. DisneyQuest is a good place to spend time when the weather's really hot or rainy. Or if you just love games.

Reader Tip

"Expect a long line for CyberSpace Mountain at DisneyQuest. It's very popular!"

**Veronica (age 11)
Bloomington, IN**

Walt Disney World Resorts

There are more than 20 different resorts on Walt Disney World property. There are so many hotel rooms that you could stay in a different one every night for 68 years! Just like the rides at the parks, each of the resorts has its own special theme. And all of the resorts are fun to stay at. But they are fun to visit, too. So if you have time, you might want to stop by some of them — to have a meal or just to enjoy the atmosphere.

Resorts near the
Magic Kingdom

Contemporary

This was the first Walt Disney World hotel. It looked very modern when it was built in 1971 (that's how it got its name). When it opened, it had a talking elevator and a monorail station right in the middle of it. It still has the monorail today, plus an arcade and Chef Mickey's — one of the best character restaurants at Walt Disney World.

Contemporary Tip
In the center of the resort is a mural that's 90 feet tall. There are colorful pictures of children and animals all over it. One of the goats has five legs. See how long it takes you to spot him!

Fort Wilderness

Stay in a camper or a cabin at this pretty wooded campground. This resort has many activities. You can go for a wagon ride, visit a pony farm, or take a trip through the woods on a horse. At night, Chip and Dale sometimes roast marshmallows by a campfire. This is also home to a popular dinner show called the Hoop-Dee-Doo Musical Revue.

Fort Wilderness Tip
There are lots of trees in the woods of Fort Wilderness. But there's only one famous tree stump. It was once called the Lawn Mower Tree. You'll know why when you see it.

Grand Floridian

This elegant hotel looks like a huge mansion from the early 1900s. At first, it seems to be for adults, but it's also fun for kids. There may be activities like storytelling and crafts. Or you can sit in a comfy chair and listen to a band play in the lobby. There are two pools: one is surrounded by roses and the other has a waterfall. There is a cool splash zone, too. The monorail has a station here.

Grand Floridian Tip

At Christmas-time, the Grand Floridian lobby is home to a giant gingerbread house. It's made of real gingerbread — and so big that grown-up people can fit inside!

The Monorail

The monorail connects the Magic Kingdom with the Contemporary, Polynesian, and Grand Floridian resorts. It's also the best way to get from the Magic Kingdom to Epcot or the Transportation and Ticket Center.

PHOTO BY JILL SAFRO

Polynesian

The plants and trees at this hotel make it look like a tropical island. The greenery and waterfalls in the main building make the setting seem real even when you're indoors. There's a pool that looks like a volcano that's about to erupt, and a pretty beach to relax on. The monorail makes a stop here, too.

Polynesian Tip

Join the Big Kahuna in welcoming the night at the torch-lighting ceremonies (Tuesday through Saturday). Before the torches are lit, there is a flame-twirling act. It's terrific!

Wilderness Lodge

With its log columns and totem poles, this hotel looks like a national park from the American Northwest. The fireplaces and rocking chairs in the main building make you feel right at home. Outside, there's an erupting geyser and a pool that looks like it's part of a hot spring. There are so many Hidden Mickeys here that there's even a tour and contest to see how many you can find.

Wilderness Lodge Tip

Look for the "Proterozoic Fossils and Minerals" display. It's a key to the rocky strata of the giant Grand Canyon fireplace in the main lobby.

Resorts near Epcot and Disney's Hollywood Studios

BoardWalk

This hotel is designed to look the way Atlantic City, New Jersey, once did. Just like on an old-fashioned boardwalk, there are games and snack stands here for everyone to enjoy.

You can rent a special bicycle built for four or swim in a pool that looks like an amusement park.

BoardWalk Tip

Look for a crystal globe under a chandelier in the main building. It is a time capsule that will be opened on Walt Disney World's 50th anniversary — October 1, 2021.

Port Orleans French Quarter

The special details at this hotel make it look like New Orleans, Louisiana. There's a long river and a fun pool with a curving dragon waterslide.

French Quarter Tip

After taking a dip in the French Quarter pool, you might want to check out the pool at Port Orleans Riverside. You can get there by walking or taking a Walt Disney World bus. Be sure to take your parents with you!

Caribbean Beach

Happy and colorful, this hotel looks like resorts on some Caribbean islands. You can have fun in the sun all day at its beaches, pools, and playgrounds. A bunch of the rooms here have a pirate theme. And there is a cool, interactive splash area and slide at the pool.

Caribbean Beach Tip
Don't worry about packing a sand bucket or shovel — the kids' meals at the food court come with them.

Reader Tip
"The TVs in Disney hotel rooms have a channel that's all about Disney World. Don't miss it!"
Nicholas (age 9)
Mount Pleasant, SC

Port Orleans Riverside

This hotel used to be called Dixie Landings. The name has changed, but the hotel's buildings still look like mansions and country homes from the Old South. The food court is designed after a cotton mill, and it has a real waterwheel that is 30 feet tall.

Riverside Tip
If you like to fish, head down to the Ol' Fishin' Hole. The resort has poles to rent and worms to buy.

Old Key West

The town houses that make up this resort have all the comforts of home. The palm trees and sunny design make it a very warm and welcoming place. And the pool has an awesome slide!

Old Key West Tip
Kids ages 5 through 12 can sign up for an un-birthday party. You will enjoy the games and the doughnuts that come with it.

Pop Century Resort

The twentieth century might be over, but it's hard to forget at this humongous hotel. Giant icons (like cell phones and jukeboxes) decorate the buildings. The hotel pays tribute to each decade from the 1950s to the 1990s.

Pop Century Tip
On hot days, cool off by splashing around in the hotel's interactive fountains.

Swan and Dolphin

You can't miss the dolphin and swan statues that sit on top of these two hotels — they are gigantic. Together, the hotels have lots to do and many restaurants. You can walk to Epcot, Disney's Hollywood Studios, and the BoardWalk resort from both hotels.

Swan and Dolphin Tip
There are 250 swan and dolphin statues at this resort. Some are big, but some are very small. See how many you can spot.

Saratoga Springs Resort & Spa

This hotel is designed to look like upstate New York in the late 1800s. There are lots of pretty gardens to look at. But the best views come from a special lakeside spot. From there you can see the lights of Downtown Disney.

Saratoga Springs Tip
The pool area has a special water-spray play area with lots of squirting fountains. It's just for kids!

PHOTO BY JILL SAFRO

Yacht and Beach Club

These two connected hotels are designed after the homes near the beaches of Massachusetts. Even the pool makes it feel as if you're at the beach — the bottom is covered with sand.

Yacht and Beach Club Tip
Be sure to bring your sneakers. One of the best parts about staying here is that you can walk to Epcot, Disney's Hollywood Studios, and BoardWalk.

Art of Animation

This resort is a celebration of Disney animation. So if you are a fan of *The Little Mermaid*, *The Lion King*, *Finding Nemo*, and *Cars*, you are going to love it here. Be sure to look up — there are tons of giant character statues. Pretty cool!

Art of Animation Tip
Kids love the pools at this resort. Don't miss the awesome splash zone in the Finding Nemo Courtyard. It's a great place to have fun with a younger brother or sister.

Resorts near
Animal Kingdom

All-Star Resorts

There are three All-Star resorts, and each of them has its own theme — sports, music, or movies. It's easy to tell which All-Star you are visiting because they have giant icons that are even bigger than the buildings. At All-Star Music, look for the big cowboy boots. A huge football helmet means you are at All-Star Sports. And when you see a 38-foot-tall Buzz Lightyear, there's no doubt you're at All-Star Movies.

> ### All-Star Tip
> There are a whole lot of Hidden Mickeys to hunt for. Start your search at the main statue in each of the resorts.

Coronado Springs

The land at this hotel looks like parts of the southwestern United States and Mexico. The buildings are the color of clay. There's a pool that looks like an ancient pyramid, with a slide that passes under a spitting jaguar. Beside it is a sandbox with ancient treasures waiting to be uncovered.

> ### Coronado Springs Tip
> Some of the food at the restaurant here might be new to you. If you don't like Mexican food, be sure to order from the kids' menu.

Reader Tip

"If you stay at a Disney hotel, make sure to ask for a wake-up call. It's usually Mickey Mouse or Stitch."

Raquel (age 7)
Miami, FL

Animal Kingdom Lodge

Creatures like giraffes, zebras, gazelles, and beautiful birds live near this hotel. The trees and animals make it seem as if the resort is set in a real African savanna. A giant mud fireplace and thatched roofs add to the feeling that you are at a big campsite in Africa.

Animal Kingdom Lodge Tip

Almost all of the rooms have excellent views of the animals. But if you want an even closer look, remember to bring a pair of binoculars from home.

Disney Cruise Line

Set sail on a Disney ship with Mickey and his friends. You can visit Walt Disney World for a few days and then cruise to the Caribbean. There you can explore Disney's private island, Castaway Cay. Each ship has special activity areas, pools, and programs just for kids, so you can do your own thing while your parents relax.

Restaurants

Eating at Walt Disney World can be as much fun as riding Splash Mountain (well, almost as much fun!). Here are our suggestions for the best spots in each theme park to head to for your favorite foods.

HOT TiP!

There are lots of healthy and delicious menu choices for kids at Disney World. Just look for this symbol:

Magic Kingdom
Best Places for Favorite Foods

Candy and crispie treats	Main Street Confectionery
Chicken nuggets	Cosmic Ray's Starlight Cafe
Cookies	Main Street Confectionary
Fruit	Liberty Square Market
Hamburgers	Pecos Bill Cafe
Hot dogs	Casey's Corner
Ice cream	Plaza Ice Cream Parlor
LeFou's Brew (apple slush drink)	Gaston's Tavern
Macaroni and cheese	Columbia Harbour House
Pizza	Pinocchio Village Haus
Pretzels	Fantasyland Pretzel Stand (in Storybook Circus)
Turkey legs	Frontierland Turkey Leg Cart
Veggie burgers	Cosmic Ray's Starlight Cafe

Epcot
Best Places for Favorite Foods

Candy . . . . Karamell-Küche (in Germany)
Chicken nuggets . . . . Electric Umbrella (in Future World)
Egg rolls . . . . Lotus Blossom Cafe (in China)
Fruit . . . . Sunshine Seasons (in The Land)
Hamburgers . . . . Electric Umbrella (in Future World)
Ice cream . . . . L'Artisan des Glaces (in France)
Macaroni and cheese . . . . Sunshine Seasons (in The Land)
Pastries . . . . Les Halles Boulangerie Patisserie (in France)
Peanut butter and jelly sandwiches . . . Sunshine Seasons (in The Land)
Pizza . . . . Via Napoli (in Italy)
Pretzels . . . . Fife and Drum Tavern (in American Adventure)
Spaghetti . . . . Tutto Italia (in Italy)
Tacos . . . . La Cantina de San Angel (in Mexico)

Disney's Hollywood Studios
Best Places for Favorite Foods

Caramel apples . . . . Sweet Spells
Cookies . . . . The Writer's Stop
Fruit . . . . Anaheim Produce (in the Sunset Ranch Market)
Hamburgers . . . . Backlot Express
Hot dogs . . . . Fairfax Fare (in the Sunset Ranch Market)
Macaroni and cheese . . . . Hollywood and Vine
Chocolate milk shakes . . . . Min and Bill's Dockside Diner
Pastries . . . . Starring Rolls Cafe
Peanut butter and jelly sandwiches . . . . Studio Catering Co.
Pizza . . . . Toy Story Pizza Planet
Spaghetti . . . . Mama Melrose's Ristorante Italiano
Turkey legs . . . . . . Toluca Legs Turkey Co. (in the Sunset Ranch Market)
Veggie burgers . . . Rosie's All-American Cafe (in the Sunset Ranch Market)

HOT TiP!
Most restaurants have special menus for kids. Just ask!

Disney's Animal Kingdom
Best Places for Favorite Foods

Barbecued ribs . . . . Flame Tree Barbecue

Candy . . . . Chester and Hester's Dinosaur Treasures

Chicken nuggets and fries . . . . Restaurantosaurus

Cookies . . . . Kusafiri Coffee Shop and Bakery

Egg rolls . . . . Yak and Yeti

Fruit . . . . Harambe Fruit Market

Grilled cheese . . . . Rainforest Cafe

Hamburgers . . . . Restaurantosaurus

Hot dogs . . . . Restaurantosaurus

Ice cream . . . . Anandapur Ice Cream

Pizza . . . . Pizzafari

Turkey legs . . . . Trilo-Bites

Veggie burgers. . . . . Rainforest Cafe

Eating with the Characters

Kids of all ages enjoy eating with the characters. It's one of the best ways to see your favorite Disney stars. They will come right up to your table to meet you. Bring a camera because the characters are also happy to pose for photos. And don't forget your pen so you can collect some autographs.

Each of the theme parks has at least one restaurant that invites the characters over. Many of the resorts have character meals, too. They are very popular, so no matter which restaurant your family chooses, it's a good idea to make reservations ahead of time. Ask a parent to call 407-WDW-DINE (939-3463).

Character meals aren't fun just because you get to see the characters. They're also special because the food is yummy! Picky eaters may prefer one of the buffets — with so much to choose from, you're sure to find something you like.

Dinner Shows

Hoop-Dee-Doo Musical Revue

Entertainers sing, dance, and tell jokes while you chow down on chicken, ribs, and veggies. The jokes are silly, but everyone always has a good time. That's probably why the Hoop-Dee-Doo is the most popular dinner show in Walt Disney World!

Mickey's Backyard Barbecue

Mickey's having a barbecue, and you are welcome to join the fun. You can eat all the chicken, hamburgers, hot dogs, barbecued ribs, and dessert you want, while a live band plays country music. There's also a show for kids, games, and dancing with the Disney characters.

The Spirit of Aloha

Aloha! That means "hello" (and "good-bye") in Hawaiian. You'll hear it a lot at this show. Performers do the hula and other Hawaiian dances, while servers dish out Polynesian food.

Reservations for all of these shows should be made before you arrive at Walt Disney World. Your parents can call 407-WDW-DINE (939-3463).

Magical Memories

The fun doesn't have to end when your vacation does. Use these pages to preserve your Disney memories.

These are the people I vacationed with:

I arrived at Walt Disney World on:

_____
(month/day/year)

I stayed for _____ days.

My first day at Walt Disney World I went to:

I traveled to Walt Disney World by:

[ ] car
[ ] plane
[ ] bus
[ ] boat
[ ] train

The name of our hotel was:

I went on this ride first:

My usual bedtime is _____ **o'clock.**

During my trip, the latest I went to bed was _____ **o'clock.**

The earliest I woke up was _____ **o'clock.**

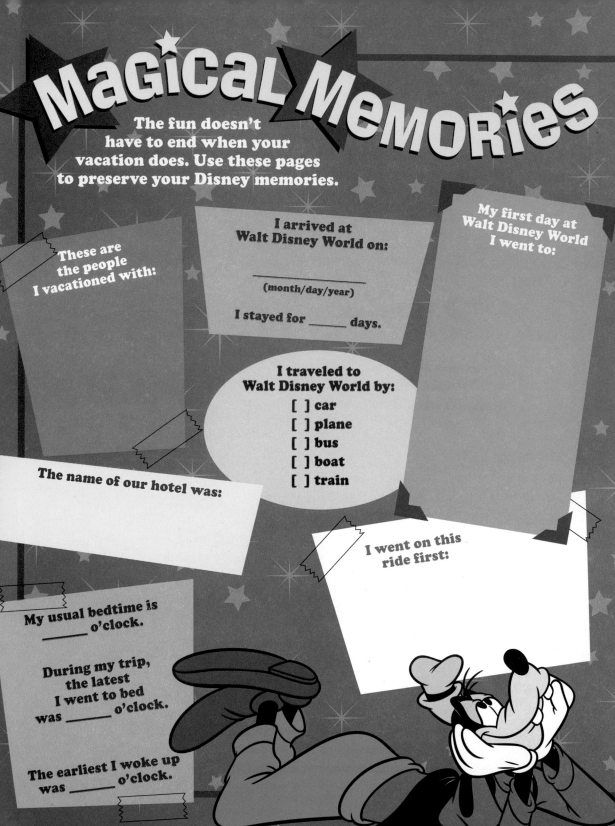

Draw your favorite Disney character here!

The weather at Walt Disney World was:
[ ] sunny
[ ] rainy
[ ] windy
[ ] chilly
[ ] snowy

This attraction wasn't what I expected:

It surprised me because it was:

The scariest ride I went on was:

My favorite ride was:

I went on it _____ times.

Tape a used Walt Disney World ticket or a receipt here!

If I were an Imagineer, this is the ride I would design!

My least favorite ride was:

I didn't like it because it was:

Magical Memories

The best Disney theme park was:
[ ] Magic Kingdom
[ ] Epcot
[ ] Disney's Hollywood Studios
[ ] Disney's Animal Kingdom

Vacations aren't just fun, they're educational, too! One thing that I learned at Walt Disney World is:

My favorite restaurant was:

I ate:

Building a theme park was Walt Disney's dream. What's your dream?

The funniest thing that happened at Walt Disney World was:

Paste a Walt Disney World vacation photo here!

I found _____ Hidden Mickeys.

The best
Walt Disney World
snack is:

I met _____ characters
during my vacation.

The first character I saw was:

Tape the corner of a
Walt Disney World
napkin here!

It's fun to remember a vacation with souvenirs.
One souvenir I brought back is:

Tape a
Walt Disney World
receipt here!

My favorite character is:

Someday, I'll go back to Walt Disney World.
The first thing I'll do when I get there is:

141

Autographs

Disney characters love to sign autographs. Bring a big pen and ask them to sign these pages for you. Have a parent snap a picture and paste it beside the autograph. That will help you remember the magical moment!

 Mickey Mouse

Mickey and me!
(paste photo here)

Autographs

Minnie Mouse

Minnie and me!
(paste photo here)

Autographs

Goofy

Goofy and me!
(paste photo here)

Autographs

Donald Duck

Donald and me!
(paste photo here)

Autographs

Tinker Bell

Tink and me!
(paste photo here)

Autographs

Autographs

Autographs